A WALK TO ROME

Dennis Larkin

TRINITY COMMUNICATIONS
MANASSAS, VIRGINIA

ISBN   0-937495-21-2, paper
        0-937495-20-4, cloth

*These pages are offered in honor of my
parents, who have gone ahead only a little
ways; for my wife, Jean, who gives me life;
and to our children, who will replace us
when we have gone ahead just a little ways.*

I am a Pilgrim of the Holy Sepulchre. I take up the staff of those ancient travellers who believed in the infallible fulfillment of the Word of God.

Leon Bloy

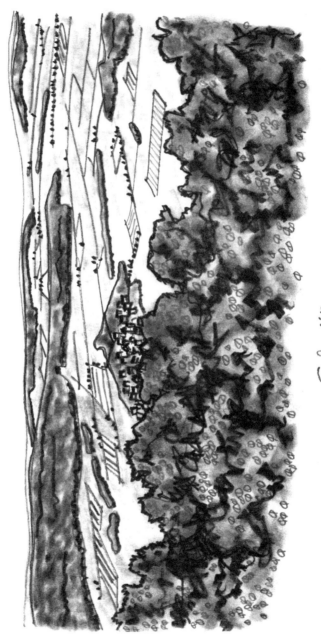

They tell me that this lovely world is ending.

"It won't be long now. The End is coming. Soon it'll be all over. There's too much pollution and not enough room; too many people, and not enough ozone. The lights are goin' out." That's what they say.

Since it's thought by the experts that the world is really ending, a writer should get moving. There'll be no more publications once the End comes. We'll have to make do with whatever livelihood we've gotten together beforehand. There won't be any new books after the End. Any book you've written had better be published before then. A fellow can't publish in any too much of a rush now. And so you hold this book.

"How strange," you say, "that your book begins with the End. It's odd, letting the cat out of the bag right away. It's so unprogressive to begin with the End like that."

But don't misunderstand. The End of the world is one thing, the end of my book is another. That will be a long time coming.

And if it's progress you want, it's progress you'll get. Real progress. The genuine article. I mean the primary form of human progress. I'm talking locomotion. Such genuine progress, here before the End comes, is what this volume is about.

My book concerns a walk I made. I walked across Europe, and this is the story. But more than a walk, I made a pilgrimage—on foot, to Rome. I've written about it here so you could share in it and be edified. For how else are we to be happy in this old world if not together?

Yourself: What are you, some kind of religious fanatic?

Myself: Not at all. I'm just the latest in a very long tradition of pilgrims, to Rome and many other places, for any of a dozen reasons. My own reason for pilgrimage was gratitude for a favor granted. Those who went before me have all had reasons of their own. We've all taken to the road with causes, and results, as varied as our routes.

Before I started to walk I read accounts of other pilgrimages so that I had a good notion of what to do. There was Chaucer to read, of course, and Belloc's *Path to Rome* from 1902. Then I read how St. Francis walked to Rome to get approval for his little band. I studied Peguy, who only walked to Chartres, and Villon who walked to Rome; but you can't believe everything Villon writes. I found *The Pilgrim's Way* by that anonymous holy Russian and I learned from it. And then there was St. Somebody-or-other who was the first pilgrim. I got an account of Charlemagne's twin trips to Rome. Also I read from Leon Bloy, pilgrim of another sort, Pilgrim of the Absolute. All of them were Bohemians of the Holy Ghost, Tramps of the Consoler. From them I learned how the thing was done by those who do things.

When I'd read, and delayed, and read a little more, and generally dodged life as best I could, the day came and I set out to pay my debt. What became of me in more than 750 miles is told in this book.

You'll learn that I was blistered, drenched, toasted with wine, scuffed, disapproved of, ridiculed, propositioned, starved, angered, deluded, vexed, enchanted, contradicted, stared at, tempted, misdirected, ignored, charmed, muddied, taken a poor view of, stuffed, elated, splashed, baked, turned away, spooked, poisoned, admired, edified, frisked, entertained, shortchanged, interviewed, cut, wearied, evil-eyed, tapped for a loan, strafed, upended, exhausted, confused, guided, complimented, and ruined; also, dogs were loosed on me.

Because of my affection for you I've taken care to write according to the rules. I've corrected my penchant for comma splash. I've constructed my clauses handsomely and thus rescued them from the no-man's-land between sentences and phrases. Cohesion-builders have been employed, and tearers-down removed, that what I've written might not go to pieces. Notice also my clever use of paragraph hooks. The paragraphs themselves have taken on their shapes as I designed them and not as the Fates deposited them. Each of my paragraphs has a subject (since topics and other foggy things simply will not do), and every subject is ringed from ankles to chin with one or more restrictions as the case requires. Strung out every which way from these restrictions are my examples: neat, clean, and adept, well-formed, gracious, and wise. My paragraphs, you'll see, present themselves as great maypoles, with subjects erect at the center and examples running riot on the lawn of my prose. You'll like my paragraphs.

This then is the book you hold, this rhapsody of one man's walk to Rome. Come along and learn what happened to me. Read the prose and skip the songs if they're familiar. As for the drawings, they were simply done to show you this part of the world as God would have made it if God had made the world of pencil and paper. Don't let the drawings bother you.

Come along with me, Yourself, and learn what happened during those few good days when a happy man made his way to Rome.

Yourself: Excuse me, but I have a question.

Myself: Certainly.

Yourself: This pilgrimage of yours: it's symbolic of an interior spiritual journey is it? of a journey of self discovery? of a quest and an inner vision . . .

Myself: That word gives me the willies.

Yourself: What word?

Myself: Symbolic. The world and everything God put in it is sacramental, not symbolic. Remember that and you won't go far wrong. Symbolic acts and lives are rarely worth the bother.

Yourself: I'm not sure I understand. What else could a pilgrimage be?

Myself: Well then, let me put it this way. Within the context of the pilgrimage process, walking-to-Rome-wise that is, the period will be a non-traditional, active and creative learning interchange. I perceive that my progression through Europe will trigger an upbeat, sharing experience with both caring and hardliner personnel. I look forward to a maximized bonding with the indigenous populations, and the mutual facilitating of quality time. There'll be a transition to the experiential mode, if you will, and an expansion in terms of my horizons, as well as an update of my pilgriming skills. And I'm betting there'll be an interesting interplay between the stress of the walk and my type-B personality. The raising of my consciousness and the encountering of a positive faith experience I anticipate as a potential consequence of key dialogings and meaningful, quality relationships which I will finalize via my interfacings with others. This long-term commitment to excellence and to change will entail a sensitized awareness of my interdependence with the people's ecosystem and the vibes of the biosphere. Thus, by experiencing a growing sense of community with the evolving dimensions of the viable millieu . . .

Yourself: Ah, give it a rest. That's nothing but doubletalk.

Myself: I can relate to that. And I appreciate your input. But I must be fair. You will find some symbols in this book.

Yourself: Aha!

Myself: Symbols such as the following will appear.

Yourself: Your trees look like clouds.

Myself: Basta! Enough. Let's be companions to one another. And let's remember what Pascal said: that no man is as happy as the true Christian, nor as reasonable, nor as virtuous, nor as worthy of love.

Yourself: You know, I once knew a man who took a trip.

Myself: Hush!

The altmuhle

The Altmuhle was still, as the others were asleep. Quietly, so as not to waken them, I stepped down the stone stairs from my loft in the old half-timbered millhouse, then came across the tiles to the door. I slipped the latch, and came out into the weak mist of a gray dawn. Leaning my pack against the house I began a final inventory.

"Auf wiedersehen, und Gutte Fahrt," called the *hausfrau* from her window above. I smiled and thanked her, a little surprised to find her awake this early.

"You are walking there always on foot?" she asked, her hair in a scarf.

"Yes, always on foot, however long it takes."

She smiled and shook her head, scolding me playfully.

As I was satisfied with the look of my pack I swung it upwards and onto my shoulders. I set my old blue cap and looked about me at the fresh day.

There were two ways to go from that 16th Century millhouse in Schesslitz: to Schweisdorf (the street being named *Schweisdorferstrasse*); or to Rome, with a lot of other places packed between. That dim July morning, on the Feast of St. Thomas the doubter, I joined the famous company that had gone before me, and prefigured all of you who'll follow: I stepped off manfully with my left foot toward Rome.

Though Germans are early risers in their little villages, none were to be seen as I made my way along the tiny stream, which also ran beneath my bedroom window, and which often held trout. Past the parish church I came, and into the village. One or two were stirring there, namely the baker (whose door was open and whose shop smelled of the hot bread), and the milk-man, and the old man whose Jersey is shedded beside the road. But I had the remainder of the village to myself as I came past the shops and out to the fields under their moist veils.

On the left of my way stood two hills making a saddle. On the near one was the *Giechburg*, a castle built by the Crusaders, which the Franconians here were restoring. Consorting with it from its twin hill was the *Gugel*, a chapel, a building of the Cloth from a later age, which the Franconians were not restoring. They perched there above me, indistinct in the high mists, houses of the Sword and the Cloth, the two defenses of mankind: neighbors, yet respecting a decent interval. I passed below them, and onto the long arbor road leading southward beside the derelict brickyard. The mist that thickened the air obliged me to don my poncho as I walked. When under the poncho I emerged from the arbor, I was beyond the brow of a low hill, and no longer able to see either Schesslitz or the saddle hills. I was away.

It had been my plan to keep to the edge of the pines which here mark the western flank of the Franconian Alps. They aren't really Alps but that's what they're called. I soon found though that all the land hereabouts was soggy, like bog, from what had now become a light rain loud enough to be heard in the morning quiet. Keeping to the watery road instead, I tromped past the woods where they near the road, and out among the parti-colored fields and the lovely wide meadows which led beyond view. Though no further along than five miles, already I was wet and chilled for want of the sun.

Now the azimuth—a fine technical word which shows you I know what I'm talking about—I say the azimuth to take from Schesslitz to the Vatican is 174 degrees, almost due south. But as with anything theoretical, this should be tempered by such detours and yieldings as sense and the road demand. Otherwise you won't make Rome at all, but rather the wall of some old stone barn in Franconia. And then where'll you be with your pride and your theory of 174 degrees, your nose pressed against the stone as against reality, a spectacle for the livestock looking on?

No, a pilgrim must be more completely a man, which is to say he must be cunning. He must find his way around every barn that appears. Purging my mind of Idealism, I followed that wet asphalt road which carries Franconians where they want to go, which is Elsewhere.

the First Vista

Within an hour I came down with the road into Litzendorf, which you see in the drawing, a village in a narrow but rather sharp valley running across the road. The whole village is visible from either side, even when the mists collect in it as they did that morning. It looks as if two trainloads of houses had collided and spilled their stucco cargoes in a jumble at the bottom of the valley, with the rest of the trains lying along both lengths of the road. Here then was the first town entered on my pilgrimage, which was as yet without any incident. Padding through, I was alert for adventure as if for some rare bird of flight. But in no time I found myself beyond the town. I regretted the lack, shrugged my pack, and pushed on under a sky of wet slates.

The tall meadow grasses began to wave themselves dry by mid morning as the sun began to burn off the mists. I pulled off my clammy poncho, and stuffed it sideways behind my back. It was quiet but for the heavy tramp of my new boots, and the chatter of meadow birds that had come now into the light air. Everything was tidy and regular in the European way.

I've said that meadows skirted the Franconian Alps, also known here as Swiss Franconia. On those meadows I soon found Friesen which was new to me. I'd never had any call to go there. Since I was hungry and sweating and footsore after the first six or seven miles, I looked sharp for the guesthouse. An old peasant woman in front of her home told me that I'd overshot the place by seventy yards. So back up the rise I went until I found it. It was marked only by two metal soft drink signs on either side of the door, and by a small trellis on which a slender vine grew. It was backed into a western niche against the woods. Since it wasn't noon yet I could only get cold cuts and some of that marvelous smoke beer, *rauchbier*, which is the pride of Bamberg, beer which tastes like a ham sandwich. The woman put the *wurst* and the *rauchbier* in front of me on the pine table, tickmarking a paper coaster for the beer, and returned to her knitting. I slid my chair forward eagerly: it shuddered on the linoleum with a sour noise. I made short work of the beer and meat.

Outside, the old peasant woman nodded to me as I passed her gate again on my way. It was getting hot now. Before me stretched those wide textures of Franconia, much like the American prairie. It was a lovely, a quilted land: neat, ruled, the colored thicknesses tacked down at the edges by lanes and hedgerows. The sun by now was full strength and I started to think that I was overdressed (for the weather I mean, not for fashion). Too, I suspected that my pack was heavier than necessary. As I walked I made mental lists of what I'd take out when I stopped for the night.

Thinking so, I pounded ahead on feet now good and blistered. The sun, by afternoon, had lowered like an anvil of light onto Franconia, stifling the bistre countryside in a pall of July heat. The odors of grasses and crops which had been lively that morning were now smothered in the steam. Even the wind was drugged into indolence. Wildflowers reeled drunkenly in the meadows, past which crept the charcoal road. Fatigue settled into me as I came over the asphalt under high summer. Hot sweat flowed down my spine. That road was a wicked road because it guided me away from any shade trees whatever; great stands of them a mile or two eastward teased me while I pushed on through the bright meadows.

Buttenheim

Long into that first afternoon I walked, overladen, deprived of shade, baking on that road as if it were a furnace. When the day had grown its hottest and the light its brightest, the asphalt swung leftward, just wide of an old hillock in hay, bringing me squinting and sweating with it, down a little glide into Buttenheim. There the road breaks off toward the other villages I'd seen from the hillock. To the east, the sign said, was Gunzendorf hidden among those high woods I'd watched earlier. To the west, the road cradled a beergarden, where there were green plank benches beneath two great elms. I chose the beergarden.

The St. Georgen beer which the woman served me was full-bodied *bock* as cold as one can get in Germany. I drank down half of the first litre at once. Leaning forward onto my knees to stretch my back, I massaged my face and neck, working the sweat from the pores. Then I drank the rest of the beer. It worked quickly, cooling me through and reviving me. What fine beer. The woman brought me another litre in silence and made a tick mark on the coaster to keep count. She returned to her sewing in a chair beside the guesthouse door. Pale inchworms rapelled downward on their silken threads. Single-winged elm seeds helicoptered out of the thick darkness above. I covered my beer against both with a paper coaster and leaned back against the tree into the breezes. We remained quiet, the woman and I, absorbing the summer air.

A cheap Opel sedan, the only car passing by in a half hour, turned at the corner with tires squealing over the hot pavement, and hurried through the light up the long rise of meadows toward the woods and Gunzendorf. There in high Gunzendorf I was once made privy to a revelation of the German character. My friend and I were sitting with our beers at a Saturday night dance where a German band was performing. He was fastidious about music (which was a fault in him). He applauded the oompah tunes, and cheered the current pop songs and the discotunes. But when the band turned to rhythm and blues, he quickly grew indignant. He listened a little while, and then he pronounced a judgment upon the Germans.

"Ain't no 'rad can play the blues," he huffed, "'cause there ain't no 'rad never *had* the blues."

It was profound, if ungrammatical. Germans don't get the blues: they get *angst*, or *weltschmerz*, or *Sturm und Drang*, or even melancholy. And sometimes they sigh. But the blues are beyond them. Every people has its own genius. Beer and theory, not the blues, are the German genius.

About four, after more than an hour's delay under the elms, I hauled myself across the street and onto a dirt lane making dead across a scrub flat for Forchheim. The dusty air and heat assaulted me again so that I had a bout of heat chills. The weeds and the other short growth baked in the fierce afternoon. My spirits as well as the beer in me evaporated. Willing myself forward across those parched last miles, I shuffled and scuffed, and scraped up a horrid dust until I struck the railroad and, following its line, came in the side way to Forchheim as the sun settled below the rooftops.

The town is famous hereabouts for the beauty of its women, and for the massive cut stone walls along its northern side. Through this wall I came at the main gate, where there's a collection of half-timbered houses that serve as the *rathaus* or city hall, and then along the stucco and glass shop fronts beneath their gables. Past the draper's I came, and the butcher's and the vintner's and the florist's, past the corner shop where they sell pewter, on past the druggist's and the grocer's, and into a tavern which lured me with chickens broiling in a neon window. Disaster overtook me there.

Wasted from my first day afoot in which I hadn't eaten decently, I devoured a whole chicken and the bread that came with it, along with whatever the waitress would bring me. In the background played "*Tranen Lugen Nicht*" ("Tears Don't Lie") a mournful hum of a tune which had taken Germany by storm. As I ate, rain surprisingly began to fall, and I dreaded the prospect of sleeping the night rough. It wasn't the last time that the changeable Bavarian weather would vex me.

A plump, pasty-faced young man with dishwater hair, one of the waitress' friends, spoke up in English.

"Can I buy you a beer? I think you'd like one !"

"Thanks."

"I'm a teacher here in Forchheim: a mathematics teacher at the gymnasium. And you, what do you do?" he asked.

"I was in the Army until recently, but now I'm a tourist. I'm on a *volksmarch*."

"Where will you sleep tonight?" he pressed. "It's raining hard."

"Beats me. I have a tent, so I guess I'll put it up south of town. I know there's a field there I can use. In fact I'd better get moving if I'm gonna get any sleep tonight. Thanks for the beer." With that I got up to go out, but he stopped me.

"I have a room in the town, an apartment I don't use.

You can sleep there. It's not far. It would be much better than sleeping in a wet field, don't you think."

He made sense. "Sold," I answered with a grin. "Lead on."

The long and the short of the whole encounter is that he was a deviant. Vice, not charity, moved him. Once I had him figured (and we were already in that apartment by then) I faced a dilemma: go outside and sleep rough, or throw him out. My burning feet and the fire in my joints eliminated the first option. I turned up the volume in my voice, put an edge in it, set a glare into my eye, turned rude, went stupid, and showed him to his own door.

Damn him, but he angered me. He'd imposed his own disorder on the first day of my pilgrimage; and a pilgrimage is nothing if not an effort at sanctity. He had no right to deceive me nor certainly to proposition me. I hated him for it. Even though I'd done good by expelling him, I'd much rather not have met the guy at all.

But even he could console himself in this: it's the practice and not the temptation of vice which is evil. The Church is firm in this and correct. And even a man habituated in vice, a man like Villon or you or me, can be rescued if he'll act, as Villon acted. And like Villon, we should all have the very good sense to be ashamed of our sins.

The next morning I had the good sense (and the need) to hear Mass in the 14th Century parish church which was only two minutes along the cobblestones from that apartment. It marks the old center of Forchheim. It's all of a piece with the old town, this church, its walls of dark and fitted stone beside the paving-stone court where sit the half-timbered shops on three sides. Above the door, so very thick and oaken, there's a sundial in yellow paint with a gilded rod which that morning marked the hour as half-past-seven.

The clear windows of the church, themselves not larger than one of the stones, are narrow and few, shedding only a little light on those worshipping on summer mornings, and baring only a little darkness to those there on a winter night. The old church had the ancient but living smells of tapers and water, of human companionship, and stone. Apart from the bell at the consecration, everything was quiet and placid that morning. I was calmed. Lingering afterward a few minutes near the paintings of St. Martin, I commended my day before the tabernacle with the abandon proper to a pilgrim or to one of Peguy's peasants.

Southward out from the town I limped into land again hilly, a land aroused. I hadn't trained for my walk because I wasn't a mere athlete; I was suffering. This was proper, for one of the purposes of pilgrimage is penance. After that first day's seventeen mile march, I did my penance through blistered feet beginning with those very first steps that morning. And when I looked at my map, with Rome at the far end of a four foot line, and still forty times as far to go as I'd come, the thought of the pain scared me.

The quiet morning turned to heat early. All of bright Franconia was steeped in a gathering swelter so that in no time my march became a labor. The road swerved left through sunlit Poxdorf, where a postman's unguarded bicycle tempted me, and then on past a span of shortgrass fields to another village where the heat stopped me dead.

In the village center, which is to say in front of the church, I found a marvel. At the meeting there of the village's few roads stood a huge, an ancient linden tree, a thousand years old as it looked. Twisted and disfigured, it stretched perhaps eighty feet from tip to tip, its limbs resting on a girdle of timber lintels. The effect was that of a wide and many-sided gazebo overroofed by a skyfull of leaves and carpeted in cool brown earth. I lay down to rest on one of the benches between the posts, next to a sign which gave the history of the tree.

The Linden Tree

It was just after eleven when I lay down, but it was noon when bells from the church tower wakened me. Out of the church doorway crept six men shouldering a casket of fair wood, followed by a stooped company in black. I stood in respect and watched them file in a shuffle along the street toward the rock walls at the end of the village. They were ferrying some Catholic soul home. It was the Mystical Body in train, the Church Militant and the Church Suffering (unless I do a Triumphant soul an injustice).

The way leading those mourners out from the town was that same street I'd first taken the morning before in Schesslitz; yet this had become glorified, taking on such appearances as by other names that road is known:

The Street of the Comforter of the Afflicted
The Street of the Refuge of Sinners
The Street of the Seat of Wisdom
The Street of the Spiritual Vessel
The Street of the Cause of Our Joy
The Street of the Mystical Rose
The Street of the Mirror of Justice
and The Street of the Morning Star.
The Road of the Brightness of Eternal Light
The Road of the Glowing Furnace of Charity
The Road of the Abode of Justice and Love
The Road of the Abyss of All Virtues
The Road of the Father of the Poor

The Road of the Zealous Lover of Souls
The Road of the House of God and Gate of Heaven
and the Road of the Desire of the Everlasting Hills.

Neunkirchen

By any of these this road is known, for it's all one: the way which takes us through this life to Our Lord. It's the Avenue of the Resurrection, which goes in everywhere that we live and leads us out again to the presence of God.

There was a little town not much further on, Neunkirchen it was. The streets were tidy and close, and beside the houses I could get shade in places. The traffic, which was light anyway, had to move slowly through all the turns of the road. Among the houses there was an ancient gateway quite thick, made of cut stones, enormously old, but not very tall. With its roof it was perhaps only twenty-five feet, a height which could be scaled in any age. There was nothing else of any medieval wall left: just the gate section. I came through the *hof* slowly, paying attention to what our fathers had created, always a little amazed in such circumstances that those noble old civilizations should have striven for permanence.

They're a reproach to us.

Old things startle us. They remind us of our provenance, and that we have a last end which mustn't be sorrow. Things like this venerable gateway were erected by our fathers who left evidence of their nature in these stones, a nature of constancy and obedience, a hungering after permanence, a lust for truth. This gate was made for immortality, or better for eternity, because the men whose hands fitted the stones knew much of the things of eternity. And all the experience of their descendants for ages and ages has soaked into these stones which you can see and feel, as into the blood of the people. Piled one upon another, the stones were left by those who have made the way for us here, and who have gone on ahead only a little ways, just out of sight, leaving a trail of dusty light with their bones. Old things, permanent things, are workers in our destiny.

Beyond Neunkirchen

The lush pines of Franconia, such towering pines, had led away eastward by the midday rest, moving beyond view. Bright and intemperate heat hovered above the wide land and the fields while the valley rolled out before me as I walked. A little flock of brown and yellow finches sported in the air above the grass to the east. In that same grass men were haying, as I knew men would be haying on the prairie at home. They were using long wooden rakes and wood-tined forks with their swathers. This rolling vista of grassland and men upon it harvesting conjured up visions of that wider place at home. The road ambled onward good-naturedly like my thoughts, and I followed faithfully, pulling tall grass stems from the roadside to chew on, sweating and squinting and limping.

Over a length of three miles I passed maybe twenty sheds beside the road where farmers were displaying strawberries and cherries in little baskets, taken from the gardens and orchards beyond. All around, the farmers themselves were bent over the strawberry beds, or perched on ladders in the orchards. I hailed one woman nearer than most, and took strawberries away with me for the road. Since I hadn't thought to bring a wicker basket, she gave them to me in a tall funnel of newspaper. To lift my spirit and pass the time more quickly, I started to sing "Shenandoah", which is the most wistful of our American songs, and therefore maybe the best of them.

> Oh Shenandoah, I long to see you.
> Far away, you rolling river.
> Oh Shenandoah, I long to see you smile.
> Away, away, I'm bound away
> Across the wide Missouri.

At the end of that vast valley, some two hours on, was a cool but narrow wood wherein a gossamer fern grew in places. The fern seemed so frail, as if the heat overhead would slay it, given the chance. I passed through by the road to where, beyond, I saw Kalchreuth, which was my mark, raised up in the distance. A steeple was to the east; I saw it before the other roofs. The town stood atop the ridge of a severe green hill which fronted my route to Rome. The road itself was making in an arc for the hill's western end, above which the evening colors were gathering.

Kalchreuth

I hadn't come an honest day's walk from Forchheim that day, because of the fierce blisters on my feet, but I'd come ahead nonetheless. As a courtesy to myself I lay down in the grass which I found beside the road, under a poplar which was near a brook. Here I took off my boots, and lounged and temporized, preparing myself for the walk upwards, imagining what all the many days to come might bring, and wondering how my bones would ever carry me through it all.

When I rose from the grass, the day had begun to cool. Shadows now sat beside the elms, which I could see on the hill beneath Kalchreuth. Disregarding an earlier choice to take the easy but indirect roadway upward, I went to challenge the ridge directly. I made a short but steep climb across the meadow at hand, its air scented by the fresh-cut hay, then through a fragrant cherry orchard, the trees red with fruit. Up a grassy lane I came, beneath a stand of white beeches, through the gate of a fence, then on beneath greater beeches, and out into a beer garden on the main road atop the ridge.

That garden was providential. Grounding my pack, I sat down heavily, at one of the tables on the gravel, not at one on the paving stones, and ordered pork and beer. The beer reached me before the cutlet. With it I befriended two couples at the next table with as much manufactured adventure as my two days afoot could afford. One man in his light-air clothes, one of many eating supper there, bought me a second litre of beer to wash down the pork, which was dry for all its gravy. (Germans are forever putting gravy on meat.) We talked on, sharing what the Bavarians are pleased to call *gemuchtlekeit*, or good fellowship. Those were good people: they listened a little, talked a little, and bought beer for a tired and aching man.

It grew dark in the garden just before it did in the street and in the rest of the world. Leaving alone, I shuffled along the road through Kalchreuth, and then beyond the town to another cherry orchard, this one on the far side of that ridge. In the center of the orchard I dropped to pitch my tent. Fatigue and the late meal had left me drowsy. As I worked at the tent, the last few day birds became silent. The weakest light glazed the cherries overhead. Little creatures whispered in the dark grass and in the branches. The cool gown of night settled into the orchard and released me from the last of the heat. By dark I was asleep.

Skreeeeeeeeech, Kathunk! Pound, poundpound, rumble rumble rumble Rumble RUMBLE RUMBLE BASHH-HHHH. Hisssssssss.

It was all over before I tumbled through the fly of my tent onto the dew. Backed against the closest cherry tree, in a near light which was not yet dawn, sat a tiny red Fiat crumpled fore and aft. Beside the gashed tree appeared a woolly-headed young German rubbing his hair, stripped but for soccer shorts and sandals.

"*Kaputt! Alles ist kaputt,*" he muttered, circling the wreck twice.

Standing up, I nodded and blinked and tried to shake off sleep. I looked uphill at the track of debris gouged in the earth. He'd skidded and come off the road above at an angle, spinning, then threading backward into the orchard, somehow staying between the trees. He'd come very close to bashing right through my tent rather than into the trunk of this blameless cherry tree. Providence had preserved me, and so kept me alive for all the glory or shame yet to be mine in life.

Well now, that German took several tours of his Fiat, rubbing and scratching himself, belching (which was indicative), and laughing with embarrassment whenever he looked at me. Before long he had it all figured out.

"Everything," he said, shrugging his shoulders and grinning. "*Kaputt.*"

"Where are you from?" I asked, in an effort to hold up my end of the conversation and to distract myself from the morning chill.

"Dortmund."

"Dortmund?" It was a long way off, perhaps four hundred miles northwest.

"Everything," he shrugged again, looking around and shaking his head slowly. Then turning, he simply padded up the slope to the road and then along it, away from Kalchreuth and toward the gray countryside, still wearing nothing more than shorts and sandals.

If he cared so little for his car, who was I to protest? I went back into my tent beside the wreck and slept until a policeman woke me and took my statement. When he did I cleared out quickly.

The Faith is the enemy of superstition; it has no tolerance for magic or omens. But after rising that morning I'd begun to read omens into my troubles with the deviant, and in my near-miss in the orchard. It was spooky. I was skittish as I walked those first few hours, anxious to learn whether I'd have another hard landing my third day out.

From the Cherry-Orchard

I had far views of fields and meadows, of timbers in countryside which leaned a little this way and that as it went on before me. To help myself, I tossed off several pounds from my cargo. The going was hard from the start and the fatigue of the first two days pressed upon me early. Walking painfully and awkwardly, I debated with myself whether to press hard each day in brute penance, or treat myself kindly and stroll toward Rome like a celebrity. I'd already lost some of my resolve of that first morning because of the heat; but to stroll was still unthinkable to me.

I'm a pilgrim afoot, and I am for Rome, I boasted. *If there's pain in my walking many hundreds of miles then that's as it should be. It's vanity to think of carrying myself so many days through Europe with no more exertion than riding in a club car.* Remonstrating with myself, I limped past the wheat and the cherry trees, past the young blue cats, toward Nurnberg.

Whatever *geist* had jurisdiction over that locality was industrious. My right leg and hip pained me fiercely. Both feet were now swollen. For mile upon mile, pain raced upward along my spine. I could only accept it. A horrid little Phobia Syndrome appeared beside me a little after ten o'clock. With my mind's eye I could see him there: his grin, his head and ears flattened and bleached white, his carcass bony and coarse. From time to time he would jab a pin into my hip or swing a hammer against my knees, drop a brick onto my arches or throw coals under my feet. Then he'd cackle and squeal. I tried to shoo him off by rubbing the joints, or even peel him off against the roadside brush. But it was no use. He and I came across the uneven land, me driving as it were and the Phobia Syndrome riding shotgun at my side.

Sometime around noon the road brought me to Dormitz, where to one side I found a haven from the punishment of the road. Two picture panels near a door marked a guesthouse. The panels promised there would be ice cream inside. An old woman who could barely hobble around the freezer fetched the ice creams I wanted and left me in peace in the dark eating room. I sat there, my feet and spine aching, and wondered just how in the world I was ever going to make it 700 miles or more to Rome, especially with the Alps, the Appenines, and the Venetian plain to cross. I was a little afraid.

Once outside, a rowdy wind caught up with me, and dark masses smudged what had been a brilliant blue sky. The air of Franconia lept up again, fresh and lively, announcing rain following behind it. A handful of swallows flitting above the fields quit the air. Together, the wind, I, and a new rain marched down the broadway into Nurnberg.

A drunken German woman of about fifty who was hanging onto a smiling Turk found me waiting for a stoplight beneath a railroad trestle in the city. Seeing that I was American, she told me "I like Americans. This one is Turkish but I don't like Turks. I like Americans." I gave her the slip.

Soaked and in pain, I came slowly beside the tall black walls of Nurnberg, the walls below the castle where you find the lawns and the stillwater moat. (You also find plenty of traffic.) The Pegnitz which comes from Bamberg and flows near the walls was churning with the runoff of the afternoon showers so that it barely passed under that bridge where you cross it.

Nurnberg's Walls

It's not a good place to stay, Nurnberg; never has been. Like Wittenburg, it was a place toward which the mischievous Faust gravitated. Too, it became in its day the theatre for fanatical Nazi rallies. It's no place—

Yourself: Excuse me.

Myself: What's eatin' you?

Yourself: I have a question again.

Myself: Can't it wait? I was about to deliver myself of a judgment against Nurnberg.

Yourself: I've been wondering how come you draw so queer? You got the angle of that tower all wrong. And the sky, it looks like a picket fence.

Myself: Those are trees, not sky, and that's what's called technique. I think it's quite effective.

Yourself: Anybody could draw that well. Anybody at all. Look. I'll just sketch that wall over there. You see? Real quick and bold, with just enough special touches to keep it interesting. Nothing to it. What do you think?

Myself: I see what you mean: that's rather nice. Who's that character with the axe?

Yourself: That's you: that's the pilgrim. I had a little trouble with the pilgrim.

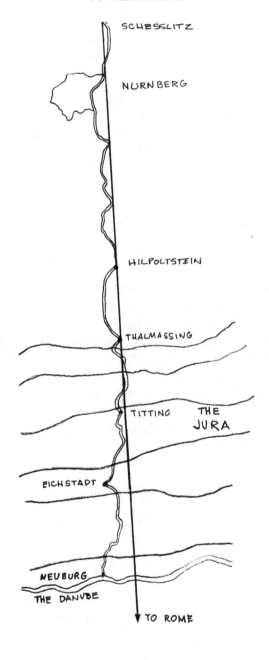

Myself: Well now, where was I?

Hmmm. Next morning it was Sunday: I was at Mass in Wendelstein, which is hidden in its thick forest beyond Nurnberg. The church was modern: an angular 'sixties construction of white brick planes all planted on a pretty lawn. I stood in the back of the church against the wall and didn't go to communion because of the way I was dressed (which was stupid of me).

The main street, still wet from the rains of the preceding night, filled with parishoners after the Mass, strolling over the cobblestones where watery treebuds lay. The look of Wendelstein reminded me of an old railroad town that has ornate public buildings from the last century. In one of the shops the baker had fed me handsomely that morning at a table covered in green linen. He had six little tables there at which he served to me and to a travelling Italian couple some boiled eggs and morning meats, quite suitable for Sunday. Past this shop we all walked, the townspeople turning off at intervals to make into the parks along the river, or else up the streets where they have their homes. By the time I found the country road again at the end of town I was alone.

Beyond Wendelstein and beyond a gray field in summer fallow lay the edge of the great pine forest which I've said surrounds the town and hides it from others: erect, imposing, serene and alive, a communicant with both sky and earth. I took the lane leading true south. The ground was mere sand but for ferns and the heather or moss where the pine straw lay. Slender, purple sprig-like flowers stood in the stronger light along the trail. Treetops baffled the sunshafts so that light scattered all over the forest floor. There weren't any shadows, or rather the shadows came from any direction. The pitted trunks rose straight and thick to the height of a strong man's throw, branching into society, reaching and stroking one another in earthen colors, the skylight brocade beyond them. This high forest filigree was so delicate, freighting the quiet air with a fragrance we all know as pine. A pair of wood pigeons called to each other in the shadowy half-light. Now and then, song birds flitted among the tree-tops, coursing never near the earth. The Germans had provided singlet birdhouses high on many of the pines so that song might be preserved here. The whole of that wood was bathed with a repose which transported any creature wandering into it, visiting the soul with that content or ease which they say a mortal may gain in only a handful of hours. It was a day for music and for happiness, a good day to be making way toward Rome. I forgot my bones and gave my soul to the present moment. I began the miles of straight lane through the midsummer woods, pressing the sandy soil underfoot so that it yielded.

Beyond Wendelstein

A local man and his boy found me marching there. He claimed kinship with me because he himself had made a five-day march once from Schwabach to Eltman. On this my own fourth day I congratulated him and wished him longer journeys on better days. They walked with me for more than a mile to a crossing of the lanes where there were woodpiles. Beside that crossing we parted. At hand there, in a tiny clearing, an old couple were sunbathing in their garden which was beside a clearing. I startled them. Whether from the surprise or from mistrust, they were no help in pointing the way to Guggensmuhle toward which I was marching.

On the far side of their clearing, I sat down on a low milk-stand in tiny Brunnau to air my feet. The smell of sweat and moleskin mixed with the wholesome odor of barn manure. From out of the sun a young woman approached, self-consciously. She was poorly dressed and shy, but very pretty. I could see that I made her uneasy. Out of courtesy she paused when I spoke.

Brunnau in its Wood

"Excuse me. I'm looking for a place to eat, a guesthouse if there is one. I think I've missed Guggensmuhle. Is there someplace around here to eat at this time of day?"

She pointed out a house against the woods. "In there they serve people, but at this hour it's hard to say. I don't know really. You'll have to ask them yourself." With a sweet smile she was gone. She was like a heroine from one of those lovely old movies people used to make when the world believed in innocence.

I went to the house she'd showed me and after a little persuasion got a quiet meal alone a little after noon. As I said, I'd been aiming for Guggensmuhle, but the owner's girl told me I'd passed it by. Never having arrived there, perhaps the good people there won't miss me either. It's a nice arrangement we have, the people of Guggensmuhle and I.

I had no complaints about that splendid morning now passing. I'd happily have walked such a wood half way to Rome.

When I set off again, the lane passed along the edge of the clearing and into the wood once more. But now the forest was overlooked by thunderheads lit by sheet lightning. The air was brisk and it smelled damp. I resigned myself to being rained on as a tithe for the lovely morning. (The Germans always seem to be preparing for rain. It's one of the richer, more prominent burghers they live with. The smell of rain is always present in these towns at this time of year.)

It rained. The water poured down through the branches, turning the lane to mud. The way was darker now beneath the trees: and wetter and colder. The going was slower too. I lost my way at a tangle of muddy trails among the trees. Which one was the way to Rome? There was no marker for telling.

Yourself: Lucky for you you're headed for Rome: any of those roads will lead you there.

Myself: If you're going to pass remarks like that for the rest of the way, I'll take you out and lose you.

So. I stood there puzzling in the rain and the mud, getting shiny and wet like all the world around me.

Nearby was a pen of chickens, and another pen of hogs. But nowhere was there any human being. The hogs were oblivious to the rain, but all the chickens were indignant. To my right at a little distance I heard a cock crowing. Taking it as an omen (which is usually unwise, but rain is rain), I chose

the mud lane which led toward the crowing, and found not
Rome but more chickens and a rooster, all of us collectively
disgusted with the downpour.

I'd resolved never to backtrack on my walk. It's far
enough to Rome just going forward, without backing up or
walking in circles as well. So I pushed onward. The rain
slackened somewhat after a mile or so.

On my right, to the west, the woods ended, standing
back from a glistening field of mustard in bloom, where the
lane descended into what the mists concealed. On the left, a
party of middleaged couples were gathering mushrooms
from the forest floor, filling white plastic sacks with their wet
booty. Two of the men hailed me as I approached at a weary
slog. From the road I explained to them my pack and my
purpose, along with my rate of travel and whatever else they
asked me. They were numbers people: Pythagoreans you
might say. Dates, age, days, kilometers, kilograms,
deutschmarks: these were the main things for them. I asked
the distance to Hilpoltstein. This was right down their alley.
One man told me 5 kilometers; another corrected him with
4; a third said 5½. They all started arguing and gesturing with
their hands and those wet sacks, calling on their wives for
verification. I stood on the road patiently (which I could do
more easily because it had stopped raining) while they wran-
gled over the distance. The wives thought they were all fools;
I could tell.

As I watched, the mist lifted and Hilpoltstein itself appeared below me amid its short hills and vapors. I don't
know whether any of them heard me as I thanked them and
moved on.

Within a mile, and with Hilpoltstein visible in the distance I was astonished to come upon the enormous *Rhein-
Main-Donau* Canal directly in my path. It's crossable only at
major highways. Luckily for me, this road beneath my feet

Hilpoltstein

crossed the canal by a highway bridge. The canal had been
shadowing me all day, moving mostly southeasterly toward
the *Donau*, the Danube; but I hadn't noticed that thin blue
line on my map until now. It could have cost me hours if I'd
come upon the canal midway between bridges.

Across from the ochre walls of the cathedral I got a
room where, over a tin roof, my window looked onto a
grubby, ramshackle garden, a garden almost sinister—like a
scene from Dickens,—which shared a wall with a weed-
choked canal. I visited a while in the cathedral on my knees,
seemingly the only joints I had which didn't hurt. Coming
out, I was delighted to hear German *fest* music. In a hillside
park to the east of town, under a copse of old elms strung
with yellow light bulbs, the Franconians were making a *bier-
fest*, an earthy celebration such as the Catholics of Europe

are famous for. There was beer by the keg (the beer of
Thurn und Taxis, a name older than America) and charcoaled mackerel skewered on dowels, and also yellow
cheeses on carrying trays, and salted radishes shaved into
curlicues, and roast beef, and ice cream. And certainly there
was music and friendship in the free evening air. *"Prima,"* as
the Germans say of the things that delight.

The crowd was still small when I arrived with my limp
and my appetite, but I knew what to do without any coach-
ing. Ordering my beer in one little booth, and a mackerel in
another, and buying radishes from a passing woman, I made
for the crowds. I sat down at one of the polished tables that
were there in ranks, joining a crowd of Germans my own age
with nothing but a wave and a nod and a full-mouth mumble
for introduction. I was off on holiday.

Beerfests are very Catholic, very Bavarian. Though not
a funny people, Bavarians are nothing if not festive. You sit
at a long table wherever they've left you room, with no seg-
regation into little cells of two or four. Comraderie and
equality are the way of the crowd. There's beer buying, the
telling of stories and of lies (we each have our contribution
to make), singing of songs, toasts, and swaying in ranks. It's
no use playing the prude at a beerfest: you have to be able
for good humor, and open to the commonality of our human
predicament. It's another occasion of the family of man at
table and at play. It's Catholic, it's robust, and healthy, and
sane; it's human, and good. A beerfest is a celebration of
that childhood still in our souls, of the right ordering of play
in our lives. For a time the demons of worry and duty are
walled out, and men and women are at home once again at a
table, in a garden, on a star.

Into The Jura

Every morning of my walk, my feet were cruelly sore. The first steps out of bed were always on razor blades. There were always blisters to open. It usually was a half hour before I could walk without holding onto the bed or the bureau, or the tent. Because of this I often got a later start than the seven-thirty or eight o'clock I would have liked.

The size of my undertaking began to appear before me that morning in Hilpoltstein. All that pain and sweat so far had brought me only six inches down my map, a map that reached the floor when I stood to read it.

When I rose in Hilpoltstein I was in severe pain. And I was doubting. I thought of every reason to delay leaving. I made late Mass; I did my laundry. Then I took a nap on a bench. Somehow I dawdled and limped around Hilpoltstein until after three, the hottest part of the day. Then I left.

The first mile of my march I knew would be gruesome. Then numbness would set in and allow me to set my stride, a stride I'd keep up for maybe two hours or more because I knew that a halt of as little as fifteen minutes would return the sensation to my feet; and then I'd have another savage mile ahead of me. All afternoon long it would go like that: first the furious pain, then the reprieve. On and on, all day. The road underfoot deserved its name, *Strasse fur der Herr zu der Wut und die Verzeihung*, the Street of the Master of Wrath and Pardon.

The way was nondescript or at least my discomfort made it seem like it was: the hills neither tall nor short, only partly wooded, and partly clothed in beets or potatoes. I saw nothing of interest in three hours, since the vistas were all narrow. In fact I can scarcely remember a thing about those miles to tell you. Except this: I came up a little hill with a pretty pond to the right. Then I came to a broad easterly valley where sat Alfershausen, and Thalmassing beside it. I walked into Thalmassing where it spreads under a wooded hill at the southern side of that valley. I passed two guesthouses where signs said *HEUTE RUHETAG* ("closed to-day"), then stopped for *abendessen*, a plain and good supper in a common inn, where she served me Patrizier Pils. I have a sweet memory of the evening that I wish you too could call upon: of beer drunk in a far away inn in a lovely hidden valley; of extra portions which the good-natured *hausfrau* gave me; of the quiet twilight conversation between two men who were friends of the owner; of the smell of that beer; of the delicious nap of the brown tablecloth; of the descent of night upon the valley.

Alpersbausen and the Jura

Yourself: Surely you have more news in you than that. I hope I won't have to endure many days like this.

Myself: Well let me make it up to you. Here, have this beer and I'll entertain you with a story about a famous American walker: the story about the time Thoreau went snipe hunting. Telling stories is a part of any well-ordered pilgrimage, and stories about a fellow-walker are just the ticket.

Yourself: Who's that you say?

Myself: Thoreau. Henry David ("just call me Hank") Thoreau, the 19th century American primitive and crank, the shaper of American thought who made a living by being alienated.

Yourself: And you're saying he was set up for that old snipe hunting ruse? I don't believe it. Even my little brother Lloyd didn't fall for that.

Myself: Well, it's one of the dangers of being a free-thinker. Here's how it came about.

Whitman (Spontaneous He) was sitting one damp

evening in April with his elder, Emerson, in the Bump, a tavern on the edge of Concord. They were at a table near the bay window up front, just like this one here, sipping mugs of warm milk, watching the posting of the day's market quotations for occasional verse and for attacks upon the Good. These the innkeeper posted daily onto a chalkboard above the bar for the information of the *literati* in the area. It was a slow evening with little market activity and it was clear there was need of some diversion.

"I have it," Whitman ventured from between his slouch hat and his slouch beard. "What would you say if I took young Thoreau snipe hunting just to sort of break him in? It'd be great fun," he continued, just as spontaneously as that. Just like that. "Spontaneous Me:" that's what he called himself.

"Well the boy's a bit too severe for that, I think," returned Emerson.

"Ahh, it's just the thing to do him good. And the rise we get out of him would do me good," Whitman declared. "I'm all for it."

Before long the two of them were out on the Lexington post road moving toward Walden pond where they knew Thoreau to stay. Whitman had the horseshoes in the gunnysack which hung over his shoulder. Emerson was loping and hopping and jigging alternately in that foolish inconsistency which was notably his own. Whitman of course paid him no mind.

"Better let me do the talking," said Emerson as they neared the pond. "He believes whatever I tell him: you wait and see."

There was little left of the light overhead when they took the path which cut from the road through the maples and birches to Walden pond. Near the water, on the grass, was the brush pile where Thoreau lived in bad weather. Thoreau himself was inside at the time, or rather underneath, refining a prototype of the lead pencil. The seer had been trying to counter the downturn in the literary market by cornering the one in pencils; but he hadn't gotten the bugs in yet. The whittling and drilling so absorbed him that he often forgot to eat.

"I've been worried about you Hank," called down Emerson. "You haven't been eating right. You look a mite puny." He playfully skipped a pebble off of Thoreau's skull. "You could use a good meal: something juicy and plump like a nice fat snipe. Wouldn't that do him good Walt? A nice snipe dinner?"

"You bet," Whitman answered. "I have all the gear right here with me: I was planning on going myself tonight. If you think you're ready to catch a good meal Hank, you can give me a hand. There must be lots of snipe in those bushes there, enough for both of us."

Out came Thoreau like a shot from under that brush, naked except for his tattered loincloth, and the two wooden shoes strapped to his feet. He was twitching and flinching like the fussyite he was. His boyish face was circled by a wreath of black bristles. "When do we eat?" he asked eagerly.

The three went deeper into the woods while the light died, Thoreau shuffling in a brook to effect the rustic. Emerson explained the snipe-hunting technique: kneeling down beneath a maple, banging the horseshoes together and whistling like this softly in the night, being ready to throw the gunnysack over the curious snipe when it appeared. He was welcome to keep all he caught, said Emerson. Persistence with the lure would pay off, Whitman assured him: many's the spit he'd greased with fresh snipe. Both he and Emerson would carefully circle to the downwind side of the wood, and flush the snipe back toward the lure. The night's catch would be Thoreau's alone. With that they posted Thoreau beneath an old maple and then set off toward the dark road, leaving the iconoclast banging and whistling in the night. By the time they were snug again in the Bump it had begun to rain.

Thoreau, being so commonsensical by nature, studied that fine gunnysack beside him, and those splendid iron horseshoes in his hands. His tattered loincloth and wooden shoes looked sorry by comparison. So he took action. He quickly exchanged them there beneath that maple while the rain grew stronger. Then he knelt again, now wearing the gunnysack and the horseshoes, slapping the two wooden shoes together and whistling.

The rain fell heavier. There was lightning and thunder all about. Thoreau began to wonder. But before he could wonder long, a jagged bolt of light dove from the darkness, splitting the bark of that old maple, setting the tree ablaze, and striking the horseshoes on Thoreau's feet.

Thoreau was aglow. He had that tingly feeling all over. Dropping the wooden shoes under the burning tree, he tore off at a staggering dead run down the path toward the black road and the town.

In three minutes he came to the lights of the Bump. Bursting in by the front door, his horseshoes skidded on the wet floor. Thoreau slid out of control backwards across the room, cracking his head on the bar front with a sickening wet thud, knocking himself cold as a mackerel.

Emerson, mug in hand, had just finished regaling the company there with the story of the snipe hunting prank. Thoreau's pratfall served as timely punctuation. Everyone at the Bump had a good laugh. Except Whitman, who was in the back playing mumbletypeg.

Yourself: Did old Hank recover?

Myself: Thoreau? Oh he came-to eventually, but not before the fun-loving crowd had pitched him back beneath the brush pile among his wet pencils. They let him keep the gunnysack and horseshoes.

Yourself: Since we're on the topic of pencils, listen to

this one.

The workers' Soviet of a pencil factory some years ago started a product improvement program. One of the first suggestions was from a bedraggled millwright named Boris!

"The last inch and a half of the pencil is only a stub. If we make pencils without lead in the last inch and a half, we can save millions of rubles each year," he suggested. Recognizing a good idea when they saw one, the Soviet directed that the peoples' pencils be made without lead in the last inch and a half.

But soon came another suggestion, this time from Basil (no relation). "The last inch and a half of wood in the peoples' new pencils serves no purpose but to keep the pencil from the eraser. It's only a spacer. If we eliminate the wood spacer, we'll save socialism millions of rubles." So the factory began making pencils which were an inch and a half shorter.

Boris reappeared. "Listen. I told you: the last inch and a half of lead in a pencil is wasted. We can save millions if we leave it out."

Then the Soviet shipped both Boris and Basil off to the Kamchatka Peninsula. A true story. Pencils are an unplumbed topic.

Myself: But back to the road.

The hills lifting up the forests behind Thalmassing mark the edge of the bold Franconia Jura where it sweeps in from the north like an invading horde of burly green warriors, and suddenly strikes westward along the Danube. Thalmassing sits before the face of the great horde. This is country fashioned of great, round-shouldered hills, rather densely packed, hills preserving castles from the ages when men would build them, with small angular villages folded into the sparse places among the forests.

Thalmassing and the Jura

The early morning was pretty and comfortable as I came up from the town. I drew clean air deeply into my lungs, it giving me to hear and feel its rhythm. A fresh heat filled my legs as they pulled me up the grades. Scrambling and swerving above the town, I climbed into a cool wood of spruce and pine, one of dark fragrances. The wood, with the daylight still above it and beyond, was only now wakening. Light pierced the canopy in places and touched the tree shafts below the road: light not suffused at this hour with the qualities of warmth, yet light ferrying the fragrances of morning deeply into the clear heart of the timber.

The birds were whistling, happily it seemed, as if they were laughing. Several of them had raspy voices. One, a talented wren with a white spot on its back, was sawing away like Joe Cocker on what could have been "I Can Stand a Little Rain". Another one I couldn't see reminded me of Richie Havens. Still another, further on, a girl bird of some kind I think, was scat-singing like Tina Turner. They weren't your average songbirds.

At a level landing under the trees was a sawmill, where the road turned left to rise again. Beside it were tawny planks stacked in a gravel yard. A handful of robust men in blue were stacking and hauling the boards that came screaming from the saw in that old barn. Men subduing the earth, fulfilling a command. I passed them with a nod.

Higher in that woods, not two miles further on, was a small limestone quarry before which stood a log barrier. But in the quarry no men were working. Here in the Jura, men have adopted the tradition of working in wood instead of toiling in stone. And fair play to them: it's hard to drive nails in stone.

Rabies

It was thereabouts that I saw the first of those paper signs nailed to trees: *"Tollwut"* they said, warning of the rabies which had spread to these parts from Eastern Europe.

Rabies, but so little else, has reached through the communist kill zones.

But for all that, the Jura makes one happy. Clomping along toward Rome over what was now a browsing hinterland, I watched the woods yield to occasional clearings, some small and a few others large, until these were replaced by upland fields under the day sun. Here and there in little villages were farmyards where the pungent odor of cattle stained the air. Steam rose in these villages from piles of soiled straw where the chickens pecked. Cord wood was stacked beneath the barn eaves. Cattle and potatoes and the common grains provide these people of the Jura their livelihoods, a people who make their way by farming. What you find of woods hereabouts are on the steep hillsides, apart from the fields.

That morning I noticed that the Bavarians pay a curious attention to the upper gables of their houses. On many you see the symbol of crossed horse heads fixed to the edge of the gable. And with others still under construction, you often see a little fir sprig fixed in a similar place. They say that the fir sprig causes luck for the house-raising, while the horse heads preserve it. And if you can somehow get storks to make a housetop nest on it, why the Bavarians are in Good Luck Heaven.

A swallow hovered above the corn and fluttered pushups on the wind. Without warning, it folded and knifed down to the field, then up to where it began to hover again.

In a side wood where the road prepared to drop between the hills, I found a familiar grove with the debris of my old battalion's maneuvers from the year before. The ground was still littered with bleached milk cartons, with cigarette butts and with bottles. The brush was still dead and the earth scarred where the tanks had gone. I walked in among the trees to review our positions.

It had been November, but the snow hadn't yet arrived,

when—

>   *Yourself:* Is this going to be a "war story"?
>
>   *Myself:* Well, yes, I suppose it is . . . I guess.
>
>   *Yourself:* For crying out loud. Give it a rest.
>
>   *Myself:* OK. With the morning nearly matured into day, I stopped in the burg of Titting for juice and yogurt, then sat on the ledge of a bridge over a little stream which was just beyond the shops, to eat and appraise my progress. Cold water and wind flowed alike down the slender channel. I was lighter and harder and darker than a week earlier. No longer intimidated by the road, I knew that I was able for tens of miles daily. There was a certain comfort in that for me.

Titting

By the time I left the moist shade on that bridge, it had grown hot. Not warm but hot. After all, it was July (or Thermidor, if you keep the calendar of the Revolution). I hoisted myself again onto the great Jura. The heat made me lethargic. I was paying so little attention that I wandered past the turning in a field and on up a lane to the far side of a bald hill in the middle of nowhere. There, in a tiny hamlet, an amused housewife beating rugs on her balcony steered me back to the road. She chuckled at me as she pointed the way.

>   *Yourself:* That was the stray coming over you, man. It's

very common with sows and with some kinds of people. Better look sharp or you could wind up in trouble.

Myself: Thank you. I'll remember that.

It had rained here the night before, and clouds now gathered again. The sun played hide and seek among them with the wind so that it was a changeable season that I dealt with. The fitful wind chilled. The sun shone hotly. Now and then the clouds gathered. I tramped steadily ahead into the Jura, past cereal grains at harvest height turning color in the July air.

Along about noon I stopped in a village to check my progress, Wachenzell it was called. Fishing the map out of my shirt-front I saw that I'd made twelve miles already, which made me happy. Across from where I stood was a chapel beside the graveyard. The chapel was under renovation. I grounded my pack and slouched on the threshold there for three-quarters of an hour. And in all that blessed time I don't think a single car went by in the street. Not that traffic had been much of a problem since Nurnberg, but I found it was always pleasant to escape it. In that doorway I just collected my thoughts and rested, and prepared myself for the remaining miles.

Before I saw them I knew there were lilacs about, elegant and elderly under the light, in the yard of a home beside my road. The scent of damp earth mingled with that of the lilacs and the linden trees, each lately washed with night rain. The uncertain heat raised the lightest fragrance from the ground like faint steam. The air of the Jura itself was still cool, so a dual quality moved in the bouquet. Lilacs and the linden and the wet earth were steeped in the mild light, spending their virtues upon it. The atmosphere moving over that land was restorative for me, a mellow tisane I sipped at every breath.

At a turning within a village there I halted between a guesthouse and a grocer's, and chose the guesthouse. An old woman sitting alone in there sold me that good *Thurn und Taxis* beer, which she let me take outside into the air. I brought it next door where the grocer gave me bread and a bit of conversation. His six year old son was intrigued by my compass so I showed the boy how to take an azimuth and how to dead-reckon from the map alone. We made friends in the half-hour I spent there. But the road was calling again. I returned the beer glass next door to the old woman.

Just beyond the town my blisters stopped me on a grassy berm. I sat there and applied the cut cure as a quick precaution while my feet and boots gave off their hot odors. And then I set out again to roam my way south over a beckoning road.

This was a day when I could see neighbor villages in the distance but only imagine particulars for them: the hogs I heard and smelled in Wachenzell, or the new brick church in Pollenfeld, or the butcher shop and the blue and white maypole in that other little place where the road turns right under an oak. They were villages I'd never visit. Both the sky and I were indifferent as we moved on. This was a silent, wistful day, a long day of yearning and patience, before I came down abruptly at evening into the velvet valley commanded by Eichstadt and its forests. And, oh the splendid bells of Eichstadt, the many, many bells. They were tolling for vespers when I took my room.

Just three bells from the university towers chimed darkly through the night; but come daylight, they and all the many others rang out for Mass and for morning.

There is art to pilgrimage as there is art to all living well.

The pilgrim is the model of man and art is his emblem. This art of his is physical art, an art ordered to those mystical designs which are in praise of God. He is as a crafter of icons, a journeyman in the medium of grace whose office it is to handle the stones and the earth and what woods he finds before him, delivering blows upon them in behalf of his soul. Molding with his heart and step, he fashions a pilgrimage by the assent of God and the charity of others. Day upon day as a journeyman he works at an illumination: at grace-giving art: at his sacramental. And things become of his soul. The pilgrim stains and stamps, he shapes the earthen miles, placing this work of his heart as within the atelier of grace. His footfalls tell soundly against the stones, some of them; certain others glance off. His strokes he renders masterfully upon the earth at times; others go astray. But still the journeyman works manfully, as in life, with the ore-rich earths and the woods, having his way with that which would resist him and stay him from his passion. Day after day he rains blows. And the road sings. One upon one the miles are blessed, and painfully crafted in the likeness of that clemency which God visits upon men. Each day, in its turn, is rendered in the patina of one of the colors of earth or light, and then carefully fitted within his artisan's heart. Over the forty days of pilgrimage, a hammered figure is tooled within his being, a fitted thing of proportion and some beauty, a rendering from stained woods and graven ores and ivory light, causing grace. And this handsome gilded figure announces that of the shimmering but quiet thing trembling beneath: a pilgrim's soul: a portrait of grace: an icon of the mercy of God.

There was no rain after Mass that next morning but there were mists, and a sort of quiet wonder in the heart. I made my way up from Eichstadt through the morning which came on. A steam rose from the pavement that took me roundabout from the valley, floodlit by the eastern sun, through cultivations to a wooded saddle in the hill line. The sky was surly and dark, antagonist to the velvet strength and vigor of the valley behind me.

Adeschlag

Coming toward tiny Adeschlag, I was led for a mile by a dignified old gentleman of seventy or more, a salesman, riding his battered bicycle no faster than I walked. His aluminum case was mounted behind the seat, and on top of it was his cane. I liked him. He rode slowly and with care. At a rose-colored house the old man dismounted, then leaned his bicycle against the low iron fence, and hobbled to the door. A woman answered and he tipped his hat, for he was a gentleman. Then he opened his case for her. Whether she bought anything from him or whether she invited him in I never saw. For I was following my desire southward.

I plodded upward in the mists and soft rains through the morning, upward with a railway in the forest, until both the railway and the land stopped climbing. The road coursed on across high grass-lands wet with rain, trailing with it a sidewalk of all things. In the meadows was sweet clover. And beyond them were fields with hop vines greening on wire trellises. And too, here and there, were corn and oats and also some rye, and sugar beets. A large dark bird, a hawk I think—perhaps a merlin—wheeled in circles high above the glistening rye. It hung motionless, it arced downward, then flapped upward to begin again. Behind the hawk, the sun collected itself from among the shreds of the mist.

After midday, my road did come down and away from the Jura, toward the splendid Danube, and onto that bottomland attending it. It was like a return to the rangeland of home. I was happy for the level ground and the chance to meet with that river of which I'd heard for so long.

Neuburg on the Danube

The Danube is a majestic full-bodied thing where it passes through Neuburg. Stone walls hem it in on either side there. Its surface is alive. There's an earthen bank and willows and watergrass; then one foot away and further below is the water which caresses the willows. Stopping to sit on the near bank, I watched it move in a solemn procession past the town: on toward Passau (which I once saw), and Linz (a city which I never saw) and then Vienna itself (which I must see).

The river is even-tempered and earnest here. It's sweet and it smells of life, which is good. The Danube is dusted with a powdery glow: the river, I think, may be lit from beneath by a river god, or perhaps by an angel.

On an island in the Danube was a jade hotel, the color

of the river it was, and below it a tavern where I found a company of eight or ten of those happy men that God makes. It's the building to the left in the drawing.

Yourself: Eight gents you say? Workmen? One big stocky guy with a bushy brown moustache? And another one, rangy, with sandy hair?

Myself: Exactly.

Yourself: That'd be the crowd from The Leinster Arms: go anywhere for a good time, those guys. Pure-dee-live-wires! What a coincidence that they'd be there at the same time as you.

Myself: As I said. They were workmen still dressed in their overalls. They were drinking pilsen from tapered glasses and slamming down playing cards with their fists like most Germans do. They were at the *Stammtisch*, where you have to be a regular customer to sit. I hailed them with *"Gruss Gott"* (roughly "God bless"), which is how they like to be greeted; it's their own affair. They responded with shouts and pointed fingers while I grounded my pack against a wall. Three of them peppered me with comments and questions about what I was up to, most of which was too rapid to catch. Since the pilsen was flowing well I called for a glass and sat at a table near theirs, already a foil for their humor, telling them stories and lies of whatever invention seemed most likely to please.

One of them recommended the boar cutlet and potato salad. Since I'd never tasted boar I ordered it. The cutlet was dry, even though it was smothered in the ever-present brown gravy.

Yourself: Did it taste like chicken? Lots of things taste like chicken. In fact most things taste like chicken to me.

Myself: I see you've had boar before.

Twice while I ate, the rowdies interrupted their slam-ming-and-punching-bee to buy me another pilsen. I liked that. Drinks and a floor show to boot.

When I finished eating, I placed my knife and fork together pointing left across my plate, that the woman would know I was happy with the meal. The stocky mechanic whose overalls were the foulest offered me a cigarette. I waved my disdain with the palm of my hand, telling him, "Cigarettes are for children." That brought a rise out of them. Then reaching in my pack I pulled out my plug of Day's Work, shook it in the air before them, and declared it "tobacco for men". They passed this around with smirks and a few wry comments. The last guy returned it to me with no takers. The ringleader at the end of the table nearest the corner upped the ante on me. He produced a tin of raspberry snuff with a grin. I watched while he snorted some of it. Then, grabbing my hand, he tapped two little mounds of brown powder onto my forefinger and raised it to my nose. I was trapped and we all knew it.

"What the heck," I thought. With one quick snort into both nostrils I came alive. My sinuses exploded, blasting my face to the far side of the room and back, six times at least.

I sat there, poleaxed with sneezing and convulsions, laughing with the lot of them, my eyes watering so bad I couldn't see. When at last I could navigate I stood, paid for the boar and the one beer, gave them a full-blooded curse which was applauded, and came out into the twilight. If we meet again beyond, I hope I have my Day's Work with me. I'll give each his own chew, and tell them all to swallow.

In time the sky darkened, and evening came into the old town to go among the shops. The evening air did wonders to clear my head, and allow me to prepare for the next day's march. By the time I returned to the island and the hotel an hour later, the men were gone and it was night. The river was dimmer; but even at night the river shone. Between those two supple arms of the Danube I slept the sleep which is in praise of God. It's the sleep of all Hope and of that of some Charity, and the sleep of imperfect Faith. But how I shall make answer at the end of my life I do not know.

After breakfast, I took a side street flush with the garden homes of the rich. A busload of young American boxers was posing for photographs in front of the sports hall, looking dashing in their navy and white warmups. Most of them were loud and animated so I chose to pass by without speaking, keeping at a distance like the good folks of Neuburg. I found myself more at ease with the deferential Bavarians than with these brash Americans.

Wandering out beyond the town on the Augsburg road, I thought about those athletes sponsored by our government, and about the folly of American politics. We have an irksome habit of disregarding the hierarchy of order, and confusing subordinate with superior disciplines. In America we're inclined to stand politics on its head.

Now the purpose of law is to form society in harmony with the insights of political philosophy, which insights are political truths. Political philosophy owes its own authority to the grander discipline of ethics—which is the pursuit of the Good—and thus ultimately to religion. It's to the servants of God through the millenia that we owe our grasp of justice. In matters of consequence, princes and politicians are answerable to priests, not the reverse.

Our great foolishness in America is our transposing the voices of authority and agency, of truth and opinion. Our judges and lawyers, our doctors and journalists and writers, our merchants clamor in their fashion against the voice of truth until the mind and the heart are numbed. Then only the belly of pride remains. The hierarchy is upended, and truth answers to opinion.

The result is that in America it's polite to be wicked. We cater to the craven dual lusts of getting paid and getting laid. Gruesome cottage industries infest our body politic: abortion mills, drug pushers, self-defense courses, hostage negotiation teams, battered women and children hostels, suicide clubs of all things, and pornography; we have divorce courts, legal extortion by banks, rape crisis centers, euthenasia; we have mass murders, suicide prevention hotlines, call-in psychiatry, and surrogate parents. In burgeois America, America gone mad, it's polite to be wicked.

How long the American denial of the Good can continue is hard to say. Solzhenitsyn doesn't give us long. Bloy said ours was the Century of Carrion. Both were likely right.

A walk in the Bavarian upland would nearly do a man good. All around me were billowing grasslands. The grasses were tall, abundant, a kind of long waving brome. High, glossy beeches stood near the meadows in little copses. On the marshes, alders grew, blown full with the warm air of old Europe. Since there were few cars on the road and it was level going, I lengthened my stride the better to make time, walking like walking was killing snakes.

Ruined Roadside Crucifix

To pass the time, I used the road markers for target practice with my tobacco juice. But one thing I found beside the road made me pause and wonder a little. It was a small, ruined crucifix only a foot and a half tall, very old and cut by some devout soul out of stone. The corpus on it was nearly worn away. I couldn't think of any reason to put a small stone crucifix in the grass beside the road. Maybe it was an ancient tombstone; but I couldn't make out any writing. Perhaps some event of great importance took place here long ago, an event worthy of memorial. I couldn't figure it out. So I said an ejaculation and crossed myself and carried on, somewhat sobered.

A workman beside the road a mile or two further on was shovelling black soil into a ditch that wove from the roadside to a hill on the horizon. It was, he said, a gas pipeline from Russia to Augsburg, thirty miles to the southwest. When completed it was to be a help to Germans and Russians both.

"Not only the gas but our weather also comes to us from Russia," he added, leaning upon the handle of his shovel to rest. "The air currents come to us from the Urals and don't stop until they meet the Alps."

"I also am bound for the Alps, but not on the air currents," I said. "With luck I'm bound for Italy beyond the Alps."

This puzzled him but he nodded so as not to press the issue. He offered me a beer, but the beer case was sitting some ways up the hill beside the trench. So we shared water from my canteen. Then he produced a horrid little tin of snuff and offered it. Recoiling from it as if it were on adder—can you blame me?—I left him quickly with a handshake, and set off for Rome again.

Milk cattle appeared now in these meadows: Holsteins they were, black on white. They grazed beyond the split-rail fences next to the road. It threaded past a few solitary farm-yards that smelled of the cattle, and then on through a genial cropland spotted with ponds. Some of this was a kind of bog, I suspected, and some of it was woodland. The farmers who watched me pass had plain open faces, and physiques that were vigorous and erect. Living on the land suits them well. I take it as a truism that working with one's hands and living on one's own land is good for us. Time was when all Europe believed and lived like that. But Europe was Catholic then.

With evening, a pearl and magenta charm spread itself silently behind the western hills, beckoning the Bavarians homeward. I came up the asphalt between the pastures to where I found an old man in rubber boots carrying a cattle prod and moving Holsteins in from the pasture for milking. Ambling cowhides filled the road between the fences and kept back a number of drivers. A dozen clumps of fresh ma-nure steamed on the road amid the hundred dried patches. Clearly the cattle passed this way daily. Catching up with the old man I nodded to him and said a kind word or two. He smiled in return, looking at me rather longer than most did, and continued on behind his cattle, their hooves clattering on the pavement. By way of conversation (since it's seemly that we should entertain one another on our way), I threw a thumb backwards towards the drivers, one of whom was shouting instructions to the old man. But he merely smiled again more deeply. He'd seen a lot of life and he well knew that such irritations were ridiculous. One car or two coming from the other direction had pulled onto the shoulder to let the cattle by. They started off again with a roar when we were all past. The old farmer moved along at his leisure be-hind those cattle, only taking them from the road at the normal barnyard turn. The drivers who had waited behind the herd for those few minutes now sped noisily past me, hurling gestures and horn blasts at the old man who gave them only his back. I liked his style.

The things I remember about that day are the colors on the land, and the little sounds. Red bedding hung from a window I passed: the German women air their bedding daily in fine weather. A little white flower, forsythia I'm told, was in bloom on bushes near the villages. The fields were the richest black loam that I've seen anywhere. In this loam grew sugar beets and potatoes, above which the birds darted as I remember. Beeches alternated with tangled oaks along miles of the road. Dark forests rose some miles westward, toward which the wind drifted gently. There were pale monochrome vistas and villages in sunlight, and everywhere a coolness and a silence suited for meditation and remembrance. In the villages where the odd car passed over the cobblestones, where there were the barnyards and the cattle and the pigeon coops, I heard the old contented sounds of mankind.

Before Schrobenhausen

The anxious motorists all made Schrobenhausen and its factories well before I did, but what was the hurry I'll never know. At that evening hour, the town held little of consequence or interest. However there was one fine, yellow inn where I stayed. They gave me a meal inside in the eating room, but most of the customers were out on the terrace, which was backed against a promenade that rings the old town. The waiting girl spent most of her time on the people outside, which was alright with me once I was served. She was late turning the lights on indoors so that for most of an hour I ate and drank in the twilight, while murmuring breezes from the terrace entered and left the room. Then I went up to my bed and lay awake, hearing the night talk on the terrace below, until I went to sleep.

So talk to me: how am I doing so far?

Yourself: Just dandy.

Myself: Thanks. I think so too. So far.

Yourself: I've been keeping track. Your average day is 16.25 miles, with a variance of 18.79 and a standard deviation of 4.33 miles. At this rate, you'll cover the 750 miles to Rome in 48 days plus or minus 9 days: at the 95% confidence level mind you.

Myself: You, my friend, are a brightly-colored fool. I made Rome in nowhere near the 48 days you calculate. Your statistics are worthless.

Yourself: Is that so? Well show me where I'm wrong.

Myself: I will. At Bronzolo. All in good time. Anyway . . .

That day and the next one were twins: long days of pushing ahead with little excitement or diversion. Germany stirred before me in handsome swells and waves. For hours there would be the rich meadows, the hops and the stands of grain. There would be the various fitted woods, the waters, the old farmsteads, the tiny colored villages, and—snap! Just like that, all the good times would be gone!—highways. For hour and hour I'd kick one foot in front of the other and come further south. Rise beyond rise would give way to me, enticing me with a glimpse into the nooks and corners of Bavaria. The houses would manifest a growing alpine influence: the roofs would be steeper and dotted with rocks, the balcony frontispieces now of polished and carven pine; the walls would prove decorated with fanciful colored murals. All that for hour after weary hour.

Beyond Klenau

For much of the day I set a slow pace, spooking the odd chicken and guinea fowl and any dogs that I happened on (but not the Holsteins), and taking my lumps with the heat. At one place, the road pulled itself over tightly packed hilleens to a yard for drying lumber: a charnel house for logs. Lumber cut from the dense oaks and pines nearby filled the yard. The forests limited the views hereabouts: perspectives were deep but narrow because of the woods. Looking at my map during the greatest heat of the day I scolded myself for my want of progress. "Walk more diligently and honorably on behalf of those who can't walk at all, let alone march into Rome. Do your part."

One of my habits while walking, I've found, is counting by fours: four paces, four dashes dividing the lanes, four flourishes of the staff, four roadside markers, and so on. I also count in multiples of four. It pleases me because I know that in this I have kinship with Dr. Johnson, who used to touch and count each lamp post on his nighttime walks in London when he would have no money for a room. Indeed it may well be discovered some day by ingenious but orthodox use of the chi-square test, with three degrees of freedom, that counting while walking is a cardinal mark of the noble mind.

Yourself: You know, I wouldn't be the least bit surprised.

Myself: And while we're on the subject of Dr. Johnson, put me down as one of his kinsmen who holds that the world is real. Johnson was no fool. Neither he nor I would tolerate those who tell you and the fellow in the next street that everything is really something else, that everything is—to use that horrid word—a symbol. For this is corruption, and unworthy of us. We're creatures of body and spirit and our dual happiness lies in the goodness of both. Don't despise the things of our world as mere symbols. Dr. Johnson didn't. I don't.

After the torrid heat had weakened, the blue overhead took on a gray day pallor, and then a deeper gray. The sky began to seem a sheet of gunmetal and shade. Just above me, nearly within reach, rounded clots of trouble now churned, low and dark and fast and silent, and full of business. A damp wind set the trees to chattering. There was ominous thunder before me. It was the look of things when there'll be a tornado, and I knew enough to press on.

I forced those next miles quickly. I took Kloster Indersdorf at the same time as the storm. Everything was wind and thunder and wet air. A bell atop the tower of the church rang out a frantic storm warning, so I ducked into the guesthouse across the street. The place was modern and large, but unlit, and so it was soon dark when the storm fell into a fit outside. Rain poured onto the street while the sky flashed and boomed. The handful of customers there paid me no mind at all, but gathered at the window instead, worrying in German. The only service to be had wasn't from the mistress, who was standing with others at the window, but from a poor rude old woman in widow's black who pitied me and put down her knitting to fetch me beer.

I sat there in the dark, sipping my beer and marking the strength of the storm outside. The customers were transfixed by it and remained at the window: all except for the old woman and me. For more than an hour the storm raged while I waited, drank my beer, and studied the room. The floor was pale brick; the slat wood ceiling matched its texture and tones. There was a green baize tablecloth, common in Bavaria, under my beer, and a stack of paper coasters near the mustard pot. The room had a cattle theme: collars, cow bells, milk cans, and ox shoes hung on the walls; yokes and leather harness-works were fixed to the ceiling.

Eventually the storm exhausted itself. It collapsed, twitched a couple of times loudly, and died. The sky remained dark since now it was night. Across the street, the church bell rang the all-clear. The handsome dark *hausfrau* by the window remembered herself then and brought me a fine pot roast with vegetables and her apologies. I took one of her rooms upstairs. With night beyond the open window, I lay down in all that cool fragrance which will follow an evening rain.

It was one of those nights which replace a time of danger or worry in which we're pressed all day long. But at last, with the night, the stars appear against the darkness. And we know we're safe.

Roadside Crucifix

The river Glonn was only a dozen feet wide at the bridge where I crossed it the next morning, but it was churning with rainwater. I walked into the gloaming across the level and now wet land, it hidden from heat by dense morning clouds. There were hops growing on their trellises, and there was wheat. Much of the young grain had been beaten down by the rain. This left unevenly coupled hues of green in every field. The harvest would be thin here, to judge from the grain that was down.

My aches were physical proof to me that, hour by hour, I was drawing nearer to Rome. I'd taken the road 175 miles to the north, and not once forgotten my purpose. For all the adventures and the diversions, it was still Rome which brought me onto the road each morning.

That day it was St. Swithin's Day by an older calendar than ours, the day when any rainfall at all is a prediction of forty days of rain. Old St. Swithin has to be reckoned with on the 15th of July.

The mist grew thick by midday, and isolated me from the countryside. It kept most motorists from the road too, and left a majestic silence and a calm all around. I found myself after lunchtime in a very mild country, and between the halves of a wood into which I couldn't see far. On the floor of that wood was a stunningly lush mohair of green, as glimmering and rich as the grasses of Kildare. The firs were few but close, and there was that uncanny green below, which shimmered with dew. In that wood, the dimness—but somehow not the mist—parted, and the air became lighter. Diaphanous waters lingered in the air, poised as a lense against the forest so that figures at every distance were in focus.

I halted quietly so as not to disturb the silence. I lowered my pack, and sat down beside it on the grass. The easy silence at length transported me into an absorption with the present moment. Living was remanded for a time, so that attention as perfect as is possible for me was met in that quiet wood. And this attention was of the aspect of true intimacy. I looked as through a prism into the secluded heart of the forest and perhaps of the whole world, so vivid, yet deep and wonderful. For an instant I think I gazed upon that door whence we are regarded from beyond, that narrow door for which we yearn, where Salvation glides in and out.

Alone in the quiet and the vapors, I considered that perhaps the wood was not so much deserted as never inhabited. In the beginning when creation was only days old, it may have looked like this. Somehow this small portion had been preserved in aspic. The wood, that wood, was fairy.

But this is not to say that the world primeval was preferable to the world we know. For mankind is properly a part of creation. It was made for us. We belong in the world. We're made for happiness here and for blessedness beyond. A man of wisdom said that creation is our Father's house, even if there is a thief in it.

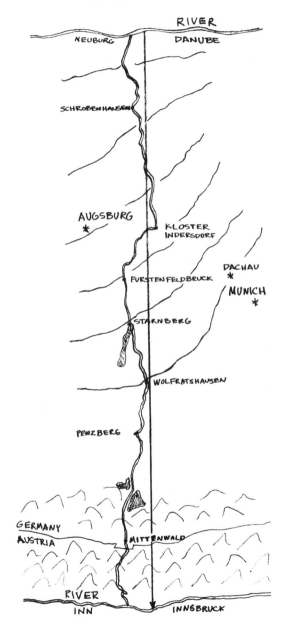

It's all wrongheaded, that glamorous estrangement from the world, their way of looking at the inhabited places as ruined. And it breeds Romantic nonsense like wilderness districts purposefully rid of mankind. Reality is a treasure we've been given. It's sacramental, it's to be revered, and it's ours. We must allow no one to make us feel aliens in any part of creation.

In my reverie I moved on to treat with the silence and the mist, and the hard and shining road.

St. Florian Barn in Bogenreid

I was startled from this meditation on finding myself beside a barn wall festooned with a mural of St. Florian, the patron saint of fire protection. The Europeans in the past made a fire prayer from their worries: "O Holy St. Florian, guard thou this house and set fire to others." Some thirty square feet in size, the mural was an image of the Saint himself standing over this same barn's miniature, pouring water onto its burning roof. Nowhere in the mural was there any evidence of firemen: no men, no trucks, no ladders, nothing. Just the saint in his Roman battle dress taking care of business. The barn owner was clearly a believer in first things first, and in keeping on the good side of those who count.

And no wonder. As I passed the firehouse in the next town, Sulzemoos, I saw a great carry-on among the crew indoors, them sitting in their blue jumpsuits beside their pumper truck drinking beer. We hailed each other and they called to me to join them, but I was for passing them by. Their neighbor's barn mural publicly reproached them. Besides, I wasn't ready to halt my march yet.

In Sulzemoos, as in many of the villages of Bavaria, there were breweries. Many date from the fourteenth or fifteenth century, and a proud few date from the good thirteenth century of Duns Scotus. You can read the founding dates on the paper coasters when they bring you beer. Medieval Germans loved their beer, as they loved all the good things of life; and beer did not travel. So they brewed it on the spot, and have so brewed it from those days until our own. When you drink an ancient beer you taste life in those ages. With imagination, you can sometimes see the faces and hear the voices of the first men who would have drunk this same brew. But as the beer in Sulzemoos produced no visions in me, I returned to my march on the road.

A sign I passed pointed left to Dachau some ten kilometers away. The horrible stench from there must have reached the people here when the ovens were burning. Solzhenitsyn tells us that the Soviets gave up thoughts of ovens, and elected instead to shove corpses whole into concrete pourings to dispose of them. All the man-killing tribes, both Nazis and Communists, have built engines of terror to separate human beings from their souls. And they must all be fought, not accommodated: fought like the Bishops fought and do fight them. They're swine. Damn them all: the whole lot of them. And damn the bourgeois politicians who bargain with them in the name of our national self-interest. Good men don't owe it to bad men to yield. Just the reverse. Bad men owe it to good men to yield.

God save me, I was furious with the villainy of our age which is witnessed by Dachau.

So, I hadn't paid attention to my walking. The broad highway led now in a mile-long arc which was the sucker's route into a wood. The dirt lane to my left would have been direct. My seeing this made me angrier, as did the horn and the strafing I got from a fop with a $40 haircut escorting a pretty blonde in his cranberry Maserati. Thoroughly put out all around, I pushed along that tarmac into the woods, through it for a mile or two, and then out. I jumped the tracks, skirted an ugly factory yard, and came the back way into Furstenfeldbruck.

The town must have been christened by a man with his mouth full—like Browning in precisely that famous moment when the poet came "bouncing up from table with his mouth full of bread and cheese and saying that he meant to stand no blasted nonsense" (Hopkins, right?). It was at such a mouth-filled moment that Furstenfeldbruck must have been named.

Furstenfeldbruck.

In front of the central church, the street had been barricaded, then filled with tables and benches. From the look of things it was another beerfest in the making, and high time.

Crossing the barrier because of my pull as a pilgrim, I took the western sidewalk and the shade. There I found something entirely new to me in my walk: mosaics: masterful, polychrome mosaics in large panels on the walls. There were perhaps a half dozen of them in as many places. One was of a young couple in an embrace; another was of a bishop in his vestments; a third mosaic portrayed a hunter; a fourth was of a bird of paradise, and a very fine job it was. Their high quality stopped me cold for several minutes. If I hadn't been tired I would have lingered on. (Even so, I wish I were a mosaicist.)

I went in to eat in a guesthouse beside the river Amper, just across the bridge. It was almost a hotel so I was out of place. There were china and silverware and crystal for table service, and an assortment of delicate English lithographs framed on the green walls. A balding waiter wearing a scarlet jacket appeared, dressed as is the custom in Europe for his venerable profession. I ordered a plate of hot pork in gravy, some potato balls, and a tall glass of pilsen. The price was too dear to order more. While I ate, a juke box in another room softly played *"Grecischer Wein"* ("Greek Wine") a favorite of mine.

There was more beer to be had outside at the fest and at a better price. (Don't you agree that I'd chosen the best route southward, threading as it did nearly every third day through a beerfest?) I took a bench in the street in front of the St. Nepomuk apothecary with its statue of the saint above us in his niche. The air grew darker and darker for the next two hours while these Germans celebrated some worthy feast or other. The street became filled with animated crowds of happy, talking people in their light summer clothes. Upon us a soft darkness descended like a waystation

on the road of the ancients, full of Bavarian grace and thau-
maturgy; I fancy it was the Saving Shadow of the Sacred
Lance of Parsifal.

At dawn, the Archangel of the East knelt, then opened
one majestic wing, and imposed it like a fan of gray fleece
over a third of the land, announcing the approach of lenity
and grace, clad in ringlets of light. From out of the sun came
a little wind that tickled the underside of the fleece and
freshened the morning, then ran along toward the west.

Marching at full height out beyond the Amper where it
runs there between its low banks, I was coming across the
last of the flatlands, past their forests of pine and juniper,
and making good time. Here was the great westward range
of the Bavarian uplands which communicate with their
brethren to south and west. I couldn't see it all from beyond
Furstenfeldbruck there but I take it to be so. I've read it
somewhere. If I were to follow these hills southwest I'd be
led by them into Switzerland and then into France where I
would come to the very Grand Chartreuse itself. But this, as
I say, I take upon their word since I wouldn't be troubled to
walk it to find out.

Behind me some 200 miles now was Schesslitz. To my
front the map showed the first of the slender lakes which
nuzzle the great Alps. Munich was but a morning's march
eastward. I was doing well.

At midday I stopped at a guesthouse where a busload of
older German couples had descended from their rolling
holiday. It was Saturday. The meat and beer were moving
fast at their tables. The talk was loud and happy. I would

have been a fool to pass up a full midday meal, so hard to come by on my marches. But it was all I could do to get served. The *frau* brought me someone else's meal after a long delay, but I ate what she put before me anyway in penance, instead of throwing a roiling black fit like assertiveness trainers recommend. I also ate the whole basket of rolls on my table—all five of them— and left myself tight on cash. Taking care to leave a tip so that she would think well of me after I was gone, I shouldered my pack and marched again onto my unending road. I allowed it to lead me over a genial province of timber and field.

I drifted slowly past a bend where the lane lifted, to where I found myself in the company of an old man, on a bench beside a shrine. He wore a suit of darksome hues, a hat, and a starched white shirt but no tie. It struck me that he'd been left there, and that he was waiting in patience for someone's return. Maybe he was a Virtue, or maybe he had been placed there by the gods. It was a long way to have walked from the town with a cane.

Bench Beyond Oberbrunn

"*Gruss Gott, Opa*—God bless, grandfather," I greeted him. After a respectful moment's pause while he gestured to me, I grounded my pack and took a seat beside him on the bench. "It's not such a bad day for walking all in all. The overcast helps me a lot." He smiled.

I drank from my canteen while the old man looked ahead above the fields. He declined to share my warm water. He had that great dignity which comes with age, and he had kind eyes. I leaned back against the bench. The old man spoke.

"I once was a strong walker too, as a young man. I was strong and robust then. I walked everywhere; we all did. But now I don't walk well." He lifted his cane once with resignation. "I was in both of the great wars, but I didn't fight so long in the second one. A shell, a grenade, exploded and I was wounded, here. Even after all these years, there are still seven fragments in my back. Since then I don't walk well, I need this cane. But God remembers me, and I get along somehow."

For my part, I spoke to him of Rome and of my purpose, and of the far places which I would see, God willing. He smiled deeply, even a little wistfully, that old man, and allowed that in his younger days as a good walker he might well have joined me. He was a Catholic, I think, because it pleased him to meet a man bound for Rome and the House of the Fisherman. He understood what I was doing, and how I had come to be beside him on that bench, so far from my home. He knew something of what it is to make and then to honor a vow.

For the time it took me to rest, we kept company: he gripping his old hands on the bend of his cane, and I leaning back. Above us the leaves of the oak rustled. We both grew quiet in consideration of the common burdens of living. But sadly the sky darkened and the wind came up. The old man said that it would rain and I believed him. It was time I left. So he and I shook hands and smiled, and he gave me the gesture for strength, which is the same everywhere. So too is living much the same among all of us who remember that we must die and be judged.

It's right that places be given names—happily, in Europe places do have names. Since that July afternoon when I met the old man who was something of a friend of God, the road below Unterbrunn has been known for him: *Allee zur Mildtätigkeit Sitzend vor der Tür Unbekannt.* It means The Avenue of Charity Seated Before an Unknown Door. The road is a memorial to him.

I hurried now. Starnberg wasn't far and I could get shelter there I thought. But the first of two guesthouses were filled and I was unceremoniously shooed away. So I pressed ahead on a cinder path on the windward side of Starnberg Lake. Dozens of sunbrowned bathers were running to their cars while above the fields grew a composition in a dozen tones of gray, "grisaille" they call it. Houses of the idle rich were scattered along both shores close to the water so that a poor walking man could hardly get a look for all their walls and roofs. I think it was to these that the cowards were running.

Starnberger See

Maybe three miles farther on, the road left the lake shore and hopped abruptly over the eastern ridge. Beyond that ridge were highlands where a large wind was loose, folding and shaping the grasses and hurrying the clouds toward me. Here and there on the barn walls were niches graced by statues to the Madonna or St. Francis. One barn held a rake of pigeon coops high on the walls; there must have been forty pigeons up there. There were potato plants in rows in some of the fields, but they had purple blooms instead of the white ones we know. Soiled hay and straw lay in short piles in those fields which were ready for plowing. And above all were the lowering storm clouds.

Finding a large blue-gray guesthouse atop a bald hillock I went in to try to get a bed. The matron was busy serving the Starnberg rich in an opulent room and dismissed me to a storeroom down the hallway where the innkeeper was working. Looking at me only once, the *ubermensch* insulted me: he sent me out with a sharp command and bent again to his dull work among the crates. I gave him hell loudly to his back: loudly and slowly enough for him to take my meaning. He didn't so much as flinch. In the hallway, I accosted a party of six coming in to dine, and delivered a judgment against that place. And the calamities that have befallen those accursed people since that day are notorious. Their nastiness put me off the reservation. It was looking more and more like a 25 mile day in the making.

That was Aufkirchen and it was a bad place. But in Aufhausen, which was next, it was a lot worse. I'd just come scowling through the gate of an iron fence which ringed another guesthouse, intent on questioning the man standing on the porch, when the *schweinhund* calmly bent down and unleashed two barking hounds.

I couldn't believe it! He loosed the dogs on me! Without so much as a word of warning.

I had to work fast. Slipping back through the gate and slamming it shut, I let loose so eloquent a curse that I later feared for his safety. Shaking my fist and shouting hotly above the barking dogs, I gave him a vicious blast. Then I wheeled and set off pounding again, hating the man and all like him.

aufkirchen

But I wasn't shed of him yet. As I was walking away, both hounds, still barking, wormed between the iron palings and sprinted the twenty-five yards toward me.

Let's talk scared. Let's talk dogs. Let's talk thinking on your feet.

Yourself: Quick! Get out of there!

Myself: The odds were against me, and it looked bad

with both those dogs three feet from where I stood; so I quieted. This satisfied their master and helped pacify the dogs. The villain called his hounds to heel from his porch fifty yards away. They sprinted back to the fence, and wriggled through again. Only when I was well away could I vent all my anger over the attack. I want to be present when the coward is carted off to judgment with his hounds. I've never gotten over it: he loosed the dogs on me!

A plain spoken man now dead, Leon Bloy, wrote that those who prevail are of two types: Fighters of Wild Beasts, and Swineherds. Here in Aufhausen, I, a fighter of wild beasts, confronted the swineherd: in Aufhausen: on *Schworenwerferstrasse*: on the Street of the Hurler of Curses.

A moaning storm line continued to build and churn over the southeast but the rain didn't fall. At the last few houses to be expected for a dozen kilometers I doubtfully chanced a little place with only a beer sign in the window to mark it. God bless the good innkeeper of Hohenrain who greeted me cordially and sat me at his table. But hang his waitress and his cook for the little they did for my disposition. Perhaps the two were kin of those folks up the road in Aufkirchen: my cutlet was lukewarm as was the gravy and it was a long time in coming. I spent a full half hour alone in the dining room sipping a single *spaetze* (half cola and half orange soda) before the meal came. By the time I settled with him it was nine o'clock.

Before bed I went out to look for the storm. But there was a surprise for me as there often is in life. Though the clouds had arrived well before dark, I now found a light breeze moving quietly under the stars. The storm had never come, though it had built above me for many hours. The example of a menacing storm forbearing to break open shamed me. When such a huge force could be held back, couldn't I have stifled my rage at my fellow man? I regreted my anger of that afternoon. Delighted in the clear night, I stood there in the darkened hill country with the quiet inn behind me, and considered this great adventure I'd undertaken: and too the nature of providence which had led me to this unnamed place of rest: and the texture of this remarkable night itself which would never be with us again.

Wolfratshausen (isn't it a sinister name for a town?)— Wolfratshausen is a town with which you can't fake familiarity. It's a little different. Either you've been there or you haven't. I've been there. It sits at the base of a steep drop where the road that has been companion to the Bavarian highlands for fifty miles at last falls between two woods. The town nuzzles the foot of the last of these hills, but it's wholly a creature of the Munich plain. Within ten minutes, almost without thinking, you've snaked down off the heights and onto the plain. The level land that begins with the town is a wide patchwork of forests and grains and marshes, with hops and water and tidy villages, all crowded upon one another.

Wolfratshausen town is smallish, and very pleasant. There are only three or four hotels and one of these is for workmen. The main street bends the town toward a crossing of the Loisach. The river is milky, as if there were a creamery in the woods above the town turning out green, butter-smooth river water. It glides. The Loisach doesn't make a sound, not one sound. It looks deep, and silver-bright. Of a soft July morning you could watch the ducks and the water birds upon it from a bench on the promenade: and the quiet river would improve your spirits.

In the breakfast room of the workmen's hotel I bought mid-morning coffee and bread and sat with another itinerant. As soon as he was served, he started binging his spoon rhythmically in his cup, stirring the coffee. Bing-bing, bing-bing, bing-bing, bing-bing. It sounded like a railroad signal. Maybe he was the crossing guard. I half expected a miniature train to chugga through the room.

The Loisach

Had my German been fluent, I might have learned more about the town in the stationer's shop where I went to search for maps. The old woman inside looked at me curiously. Yet she didn't question me while I chose a half dozen maps that had much greater detail of my route into the Alps. By now my one large map, kept constantly inside my shirt, was damp and worn just where I had the greatest need of detail. So I bought those maps in Wolfratshausen which would see me all the way to Italy. I paid the woman, and shuffled on through the town on feet that had grown tough, and legs that were now sturdy after two hundred miles afoot. My confidence had also improved in the nine days of marching. Though the most difficult part of my route still lay ahead, I had no real doubts about my ability.

But I was becoming a little bit lonely: I don't know why, I was just getting a little lonely.

The solemn Loisach's name might suggest it was named by one of the Irish holy men as he passed in his sixth century wandering. I wonder. I kept it beside me, as I pushed south and somewhat upward toward its source. As the river was moving the opposite direction, I was the natural favorite to reach Rome first. A very plain thing beyond the town, a sluggard, not up to standards, a river in the 2nd quartile: the Loisach would do well not to come dragging its dreary self through Europe.

I could see the Prealps now and a clutch of low houses from beyond Wolfratshausen—and ice fields—from that road which wove beneath shimmering beeches. The mountains were the bluish color of the sky, so that it was a little hard to fix the ridge line of the furthest peaks. I was thrilled and a little fearful at the sight of them. There were oaks about, but higher up in the distance where things got serious, there were only pine and larch. The road was still a quiet road, a proper neighbor for dairy cattle and their ancient pastures. Thankfully, the traffic was all on the expressway a few miles to the east, near Munich.

The Prealps

For the past many miles I'd seen versions of a sign in a decorative Black Forest lettering, very old and severe, proclaiming this message: *"Man Kommt Du Was Durch Wustenrot."* Piecing together what I could from my guesthouse-German, I concluded that it was a prophetic warning to the age, as in "Remember, man, that what you are drawing near to with every day is the ruin of the grave." Or so it seemed to me.

The alpine influence on the houses was certain now. That day I saw white houses in every village which had large murals on their walls, murals of a hundred different themes, but all of them expertly done. The roofs of the houses were steeper now, and made of tile. Large white rocks dotted these roofs, some say to help collect heat and melt snow in the dead of winter.

I made hard advance in spite of the wilting heat. From ten until after five the heat was oppressive, and the air very muggy. Aware of the mountains some thirty miles distant, I savored this the last of the level going to be expected until the plain of Venice another two hundred miles to the south. It was a day of pounding, of marching hour upon hour, all sweat and glare and perseverance, a day of preparing myself for the test. "Lots of heat here," is all I wrote on this part on my map. Not until the descent of the most crippling heat at three did I stop. Finding a strip of meadow shade beside a copse of what I think were beeches, I lay down upon the living grass, and there I slept.

Twice there I roused but went to sleep again: I just didn't care what time it was or where I was.

Some hours later, at about seven, now rested, I was hauling myself down a gravel lane off of a hillock and into Penzberg. Two fat men sitting on a veranda with their beers were laughing. I found them no use in guiding me toward any tavern. They just laughed and went stupid. A policeman in town was no help either. Down the main street I struggled, on the shady side for comfort, and aching a little from hunger. I came to a stop-light which the Dialectic had turned to red. Beside me appeared a fiftyish man with salt and pepper hair, in yellow summer slacks, his hands clasped behind him in the German fashion.

"Please, where is a guesthouse?" I asked in my best Sunday German.

"Huh?"

"A guesthouse: Eat, drink?" I gestured and said.

The man smiled kindly as creases appeared at the corners of his eyes, but I couldn't make anything of his response. I asked again without success. Peeved, I started to move off when he touched my arm, trying to be understood. Then I saw the hearing aid in his ear and knew his speech to be impaired and not a dialect. I was asking directions of a man who was nearly deaf and mute. Silently I cursed my luck, but I held fast to hear him out of courtesy. (I'm very agreeable, by and large.)

There on that street corner in Penzberg I was treated to an artful pantomime of the directions, all very clear, to a guesthouse he recommended, as well as to an alternate. The old gentleman mimed that I should go three blocks further (two of which were stoplights), turn left on the far side of the street, walk to the second door and enter without knocking. Inside, he assured me, was a place with good food and reasonable rates.

We parted in courtesy and I soon found it as he'd said. In the new hotel where I stayed I bought a very big meal, and very good too: rumpsteak with garlic butter and a broiled tomato, and a bowl of beef bouillon with an egg in it, and also two beers; and then some coffee.

Yourself: You ate all that?

Myself: You bet. Right down the little red lane.

After my supper I was content, and so I went out to the cool air of the evening. Just a few feet away stood my deaf

mute friend, window-shopping alone. I walked over to thank
him for his help.

    I spoke with my voice and emphasized with my hands.
With him it was the reverse: it was his hands and eyes which
were resonant. His voice was soft, muffled too, but I couldn't
make out any true words. He certainly could laugh aloud,
and this made me happy. I talked of my pilgrimage to Rome
and he was amazed. The old gentleman congratulated me.
He too was Catholic, as he showed by the sign of the cross.
He told me, I still don't know how, of his family and his
home, and that he loved his wife who had given him this
wedding band. She was a good woman, to see him tell of her.
Somehow we took up politics, and then Eisenhower as both
general and president. From that we settled into the single
most comfortable topic of conversation for all mankind: the
weather.

    Yourself: Why do you say "single most"? A superlative

must always be single. *Wie Gehts?*

Myself: Touchè.

I say we took up the weather. Talking about the weather is purely a demonstration of human courtesy, an effort to put others at ease with us. By husbanding one another with conversation or with any of the common occasions of human warmth, by loving one another, sharing bread, comforting and attending one another in any of a hundred ways, we preserve and rescue ourselves until the End. We do well. If you want to make me happy, talk to me about the weather.

We strolled the sidewalk through the evening, the old gentleman laboring for my benefit with his hands and eyes. I grew fond of him. His kindness was genuine, and this it seemed was owing to the burden of his handicap. Perhaps other men were unwilling to tarry with him, I don't know. He was good to me and I believe he will go to Heaven.

The evening grew late. Darkness settled upon us from the mountains. The streets of Penzberg emptied, and he told me he was expected home. We clasped our four hands. Quietly I watched him cross the road and turn up a side street, his hands behind him, his salt and pepper hair disappearing into the darkness of the trees beyond.

I like to think that he and I will talk again in the streets of Paradise, and that we'll laugh. And when it's evening there, please God he'll show me home at last.

The mild hour I spent on the street in Penzberg was a blessing. Next morning my happiness grew when, looking at my map, I saw that before nightfall I would be free of the

Munich plain and moving among the Prealps, the first of these mountains which were meant to be the capital test of my march. I swung onward happily.

With the new day I attended Mass in the crypt of a church. That Mass satisfied me as every Mass satisfies. In it there's plentitude: I mean the presence of all those things necessary for happiness. Consider that in the Mass we have talk, we have ritual, an intimacy of the sublimest form, and prayer; and glory. We have mercy. At Mass we suffering creatures have praise for our Creator, and proper thanksgiving; the Word is there, and bread, and water, and wine; we have song in chorus, or solo, friendship and love. We have, in each Mass, instruction (which we need), fire and its warmth, color, a great deal of grace, and welcome; variety is there, the touch of human hands too, and blessing and valediction. And always there is that Body which is the Body of God. And these we are given in every Mass. Every needful human thing is provided for us. It's the Most Human Hour. The Mass is like those hours our family knew before they left the Garden, an hour when we partly reclaim those many precious things from which we're now sadly estranged.

As I cleared the wood that attends Penzberg I saw, lifted up from the wide moor and in front of a stipple sky, a high range of slopes and the first bare rock outcrops which I knew to be the arena. Nearer by far, only three or four miles away, stood the onion-shaped domes of Benediktbeuern, the monastery which has long been famous for its baroque chapels and its art. I passed it by, since the cloister itself was another mile or so west of the road.

Mountains to me are a foreign—though not alien—thing. (Nothing God has made is an alien thing.) I learned nothing on the plains to prepare me for them. Upright they stood, unannounced and immediate like a tap on the shoulder, facts to be dealt with. They were to be the first of my mountain trials.

The Prealps

The map I'd brought with me from Wolfratshausen named them: Herzogstand to the right at 1,730 meters; Jochberg its brother to the center; the Benediktenwand spread out at the left at 1,750 meters; and the little Kochel Lake lying at their feet. The next map in the series told me the layout of all the rock faces between here and the Innsbruck valley: Soiernspitze (2,259 meters); Krottenkopf (2,086 meters); and the jagged Karwendelgebirge range, spelled out along the Innsbruck valley in letters each as large as the town of Penzberg. This Karwendelgebirge is a chain of Herculean rock: Tiefkarspitze (2,430 meters); Worner (2,476 meters); Hochkarspitze (2,484 meters); Raffelspitze (2,325 meters); Barnalplkopf (2,325 meters); Schlichtenkar-Spitze (2,477 meters); Vogelkar-Spitze (2,523 meters); Ost Karwendel-Spitze (2,537 meters); Grabenkar-Spitze (2,472 meters); Lackenkarkopf (2,413 meters). When you remember that one meter is a shade longer than a yard, you see that the far range in my path was over 7,000 feet high. Along these at their crests my map showed a cross-hatched line in red: the border between Germany and Austria.

As I looked I tried to comprehend their might: bulking,

stiff, upright and sure, draped in loden under the blue and near-blue morning. I spoke out loud to several of them by name, conjuring them to my purpose, asking that they and their kinsmen might deal honorably with me.

The Kochelsee

The level approach quietly skirted the bluewater Kochel where little rowboats were beached, and ended at a muss of a gravelled woodland path which led upward several hundred feet. The path was dark and close and warmer, as it went up beneath a leafy growth of trees and brush. It was a leaf mine, some three miles and forty minutes deep. It burrowed its way to a saddle between two shoulders of rock, then led down and out again under the blue, bringing me to the Walchensee, which is higher and larger than the Kochel.

Before me, fashioned in glorious wide array, lay the elements of Earth. Below and away stretched that luminous blue: vibrant, fresh, a fitting of many waters, majestic, and carrying sails. On the narrow rising skirt were villages and homes, where the daylight beamed upon the glassy colors as though they were so many little flames. Solemn fragrances

eased through the air with the barest suggestions of water
and earth. On every side stood the many: Herzogstand and
Jochberg behind me, Heimgarten to the west, Hochkoff beyond in the light, the Jachenau rising away into the east.
They were draped in high forest blue, and crested in taupe
or gray rock from which runnels of water and light glissaded,
finding their many ways down. And tethered to the crags, the
canvass of Heaven itself swung and billowed in the daywind.

My soul was commanded to prayer. Silently I lit 300 votive lamps on the floor of my soul. I grounded my pack and
stood contemplating, that is delighting, moved by the splen-
dor.

At hand I found a guesthouse veranda above the water
from which I could take in the panorama. Without any doubt
it was the prettiest place I'd seen in 250 miles of marching.
At the guesthouse the woman ignored me until it pleased her
to fill in a few slack moments. She charged me shameful
prices for fish as though I were a mere tourist. Escaping from
her mercantile rudeness, I followed a cinder path along the
western shore at a stroll. For a good two hours I lumbered
into the assembling afternoon.

Silent parti-colored massifs abounded on every side.
They were different from the warm but hidden wind, light-
fingered and barely audible, a *foehn*, blowing down the
shoulder of Heimgarten, coasting then onto the face of the
waters where it rippled away to the east. A fine spray per-
fumed the lane. The foaming of the little waves on the pebbles made a companionable chatter. Vapors, wraithlike, rose
toward the sun; they wheeled before the high rock and dis-
solved against every light. Afternoon in that stone vessel
suggested a poem whispered into a cup of fair wine, a poem
we may learn wherein one may address God from a distance
and then die; it's that poem which tells of three things that
last, things so similar to these high and colored mountains,
and so unlike us and the wine.

The Walchensee

The lake narrowed. The cinders shifted leftward there with the shore before breaking with it and rising a little into a crease. I carried on into the trees and left the wonder behind.

Wallgau spends the seasons upon a narrow floor between these high woods and ridges. At the only bend in its road, I saw that I was being watched from the Oil Can Harry side of the street. A porky, red-faced man sat at a table behind the picture window of a restaurant, watching me intently (Germans have a very bad habit of staring). I jaywalked to his side of the street. While I approached, his meal was forgotten. As I passed within a foot or two of the window, the boor's head swivelled with me. Just for meanness, I wheeled around and pressed my face against his window, glaring at him from beside his plate. Well! The boor came unstuck; he tried to hurry food into his head to distract himself, but couldn't swallow what was already in it. He reached for knife then glass then napkin then spoon then knife all over again. It was great turning the tables on him there, watching the waxworks above his collarbone misfiring. I think I broke him of staring at strangers.

In the next little place, which is called Krun, they don't deal with anyone for just one night. Those people there talk big dollars (or deutschmarks) and are only interested in long-term tourist guests. What's more, if you get to Krun, or any other town around here, between noon and 4:30 and you're thinking of stopping you can forget it. They're closed. If you ask about a good meal, *mittagessen*, the answer is a brisk shake of the head: "*Nein*."

Without a meal or a room, I pressed on slowly into the declining afternoon, a little crestfallen for not finding a room in either Wallgau or Krun. Humbly I followed the noisy main road south, beside the Isar, where all the traffic to Garmisch, only ten miles west, was rumbling. This is tourist country at any time of the year. Campgrounds abound, along with foreign license plates, and guesthouses full for the season. I forced myself south on the shoulder of the road, piecing together an impression of the Prealps from the nearest slope, the deep green meadows where men were haying, the stark differences of light and shade in the sky, and the flash thunderstorm which came upon me there.

By the time I came into Mittenwald near the Austrian border, I was perhaps five miles west of the true line to Rome. This is because I was keeping to the beaten path: I would have needed to be double-jointed to follow the straight line slap over the face of the Scharfreuter or the Risserfalk, those two terrors. Remember, my vocation was as a pilgrim to Rome, not an acrobat on the mountain tops. And if I got along toward Rome afoot I did well. Very well. For a plainsman like me, that meant going by the common way where practical. Why should I spend days hacking up and down alpine peaks when my azimuth through the high Alps themselves pierced exactly at the Brenner, the lowest of passes? If the line from Schesslitz to Rome wove through the Brenner, then certainly it lay through any such low ways as my aching legs required.

Yourself: You know, I was just about to mention that. Let's stay off the mountain tops. I'm not double-jointed any more than you are.

Mittenwald is boldly colored and bright, almost garish there on its level place amid the Prealps. The impression which meets the eye is a riot of colors, of storybook walls and woodcarvings, and visitors in their travelling clothes. It swarms with enough tourists of a summer day to fill a contract. In fact there were so many of them and so few of me the day I was there that it made me stare.

Yourself: Any good bargains you found there?

Myself: No, I didn't tarry to shop. I just stopped to pass the night but not to shop.

Next day I hurried through the town, leaving the gaudy shops and their customers in my wake. It's a busy, hurried, sunlit palette of a place, not meant for a pilgrim. I didn't talk to anyone as I hustled out of town.

The four miles or so to the frontier were delectable: the churning, mountain-wedded Isar danced below the slopes, attending that little gravel path which wove southward through the living grass and the gesturing spruce boughs. Wooden benches stood alongside the path and on these there were couples taking their ease beneath the splendors. Intertwining and alternating with one another through little bridges, the Isar and the walkway carried on beside the highway at the foot of the mountain at my left. I sidearmed a couple flat pebbles onto the Isar, but the water was too rough and they wouldn't skip. As I walked I looked forward to meeting the Austrians.

Before Austria

Beyond one final bridge over the waters, I scrambled up an embankment of rocks and walked onto the German border pavilion. The smart young guard in green waved me through with the briefest look of disgust. Beyond him the Austrian sentry in gray examined me more closely, not wanting to trust in my scruffy appearance. But nothing was amiss with my passport, and he stamped it and let me in, thus despoiling his fatherland.

I'd taken Austria by foot!

I had walked Franconia and the length of Bavaria to stand now in the land of the Tyroleans. I'd adventured a full two-hundred fifty miles. The mass of my effort expanded in my mind, and events of but a week earlier were flown backward into history.

My border passage marked me indelibly as a manly pilgrim hammering for Rome in the sturdy tradition of the Faith. What worthy folks we Catholics are! How excellent! How constant! How fine! We're the envy of the race!

Yourself: Well, pin a rose on you!

Myself: After choosing a cattle trail beside a meadow in old Tyrol, a little twisted path otherwise known as *Gasse der Schwanmörder*, the Street of the Slayer of Swans, I stepped smartly along the valley floor as fitted my purpose. Smartly, that is, until a rainstorm jumped up and spooked me into a hay barn for shelter. Two rain-soaked hikers were already inside when I arrived: a couple dressed up properly in knee britches and wool socks with heavy mountain boots. They were lovers in their late twenties devoted to one another. Both were a little abashed at my finding them there. So I lay down on the hay wagon to one side and feigned sleep for their benefit. They giggled and tumbled around and tossed handfuls of hay at one another. Then, all at once the rain ended and they were gone.

The way was rising softly as I came through Scharnitz, Scharnitz which is of no account. Beyond the village, young men and young women were in the meadows cutting down the good grass. A tidy well-behaved stream had cut a channel into the narrows between the green slopes to the right and the spine of rugged stones (the frontier) climbing from lower hills on my left. Beside the stream lay the wet highway, the cattle trail, and a railroad (this last put there by the Devil to torment the people of that valley and any chance pilgrim—as you'll hear).

On toward Rome I came. Along toward the evening cool, I made Seefeld, very hungry and hunting a poor man's cafe. But Seefeld was a picture of prosperity, newly washed after the rain as if for its judging. Give it a red ribbon for second place. Anyone serving poor man's food there was too timid to put his head out. Settling for a showy roadside restaurant at the near end of town, I ordered an omelet with some peppers and onions and beef in it. In my head I converted the price in schillings into dollars. It was right then that I started to fear for my wallet in Austria. "Nine dollars" for an omelet. It shouldn't be. Two days later when I was almost clear of Tyrol I discovered the risk of doing arithmetic in the head: all the way across Austria I'd divided prices by the inverse of the complement of the exchange ratio, or something like that, and really had had no reason to worry. I'd had plenty of money.

Anyway, I was sitting there by the door eating and ciphering and growing despondent, when a tray of fish dinners crashed down beside me onto the laps of a rich pair of fat Austrians (or Germans: I can't tell them apart). The soiled woman rose up in a rage at the poor serving girl, who hurried away in tears. It seemed to gratify the woman to humiliate the girl in front of us. I gave her a hard look for all her fuss and cleared out of there, leaving a big tip for the girl anyway, doing more arithmetic and troubling my head.

The road hauled itself stiffly up a steep height of five hundred feet, where it leveled off in a grassy draw. That draw bore southwards between the bent feet of those old mountains. It was a lovely, placid evening before a pastel sky. I found myself well-fed and generally content with my progress. I was tired and sore and looking for a place to settle. As the last light died above, I found what I wanted: a flat berm of grass beneath a long line of spruces to break the wind. There was no moonlight so I pitched my tent in the dark by touch, and then I lay down in Tyrol and I slept.

Something was wrong . . .

A grinding roar awoke me, gathering, growing, coming from every side. Everything was a menacing rhythmical snarl. I was surrounded by noise. A din was on top of me in the night. Swelling confusion terrified me. Throwing myself in one lurch through the flap of my tent, I froze. A blade of light slashed into the spruces above my head. My mind was halved by a monstrous blast. Again and again, a huge horn cut into me and devastated the night. Not twenty feet away, just beyond the windbreak, a night train roared past me chasing a blade of light.

I was poleaxed. Impaled by the fear. I was as frightened as I've ever been.

Except for the time I met the Hook Man.

Yourself: You met the Hook Man?

Myself: Yes.

Yourself: Criminy!

Myself: It was when I was a boy. The Hook Man, like his fellow fiend the Coffee Man, preys upon prairie children, inflicting terror and mayhem with that gruesome hook he wears for a hand. So you'd expect it to be as a child that you'd meet him, if ever.

Yourself: Well, I'm wide awake now after that commotion with the train, so let's hear it.

Myself: My two cousins and I were fishing on my grandfather's farm one summer evening after a rain. We had parked the car at the road junction and walked the eighty yards of gravel road along the wet ditches and the cornfields toward the bridge over Clark's Creek. From there my older cousin had gone downstream to his favorite hole while the younger girl and I fished from the bridge.

It's wise to be quiet while fishing so I contented myself with watching the evening. Turning toward our car, I saw what seemed to be a tree stump near it, a tree stump I couldn't remember seeing there before. I looked at it, studying and puzzling. As I did, it moved. The stump moved, waddling forward three or four paces, and then froze.

In my confusion I tried to imagine what could be the size of a three foot tree stump and move around in the night (it was nearly dark now and a good time for fishing, or for hallucinating). Sometimes in the summer, I remembered, black bears wander up onto the prairie from the Ozarks, only to be shot by farmers or killed on the highways. If this were a bear, it was between us and the car.

For upwards of twenty dark minutes I watched transfixed as the creature stalked forward: waddling three steps or four along the ditch, then freezing for a couple minutes, then waddling ahead into the darkness, and freezing again.

In this cadence the creature came ahead. When it was two-thirds of the way toward us along the road, it made a move forward once more. But it shocked me: it stood upright, manlike, and marched forward ten paces toward our bridge, and then crouched again.

It was a man! In his hand the man carried a long thick staff. And on the end of the staff was a horrendous great hay hook.

It was the Hook Man! I just knew it in my twelve year old heart, no matter that the hook was fixed to a pole and not to his wrist, as often reported. No one else would stalk toward children along the ditch of a country road in the dark, carry no light, make no sound, and brandish a terrifying hooked staff. Had I not known he was creeping there beside the ditch, I couldn't now have seen him: his form was as black as the night which had swallowed us.

Closer the Hook Man drew in two and three yard stalks, methodically covering the remaining road between us in fifteen minutes, until at last he was crouched silently at the abutment of the bridge itself, indiscernible against the weeds. He wasn't ten yards from my cousin and me. There was nothing between that horrendous hook and us but cool, black air.

Yourself: Run! Get out of there! Quick! RUN! Call for help! RUN!

Myself: The Hook Man froze in place, crouched there at the end of our bridge. Then he swelled to his full height, moved that hooked pole to port-arms, and started into the ten feet of blackness between us.

My eyes bulged and I let out a pitiful moan. "Oeoeoeoeumum." The girl looked; she saw my horror, turned around, discovered for the first time the advancing Hook Man, and let out a shriek: "Eeeeeeoooooooiiiiii."

The Hook Man flinched, he buckled, and he dropped his pole with a clatter onto the bridge. He grabbed at his chest, staggered back against the bridge rail, and screamed: "Oooooouuuuuaaaaaaa." I joined both of them in three-part screaming, the girl now crushing my neck and yelling through the side of my skull.

When my older cousin arrived and calmed us down, this is what we learned. The Hook Man is the son-in-law of old Tony Neiers who owns the neighboring farm on Clark's Creek. He hadn't seen us that night until my young cousin had yelled at him from ten feet away; we'd been quiet and it was too dark for him to see us. That night he'd been out to gaff frogs for bait from the wet ditches along the road; but he hadn't found any, so he hadn't used the hook.

That's what it was like to meet the Hook Man. It was terrifying: more frightening by far than waking nearly under the wheels of a locomotive.

Yourself: Does all this have a lesson?

Myself: Certainly. The lesson is that the sources of legends are real, and that they're valid. People aren't fools. Beware of the Hook Man.

The faintest flush colored the east as I rose and moved off into the morning. It was early yet, with only a gray light abroad, and I tried to waken as the road descended—lightly at first—and then dove sharply into a defile between the spruces. A charming shrine to Our Lady of stones and timbers sat poised at a diversary beside the road. It alone of all the world seemed to have prepared for the arriving light. I came past it, moving at a good clip now and going downward until a pathway appeared in the spruces. It led more directly over the brow of the mountain. And so I left the road.

The path was of rocks and it jarred my step. In there it was very hard to see, since it was still just after first light. But I pushed downward. Some ways down the mountain and maybe a dozen paces to the side I saw tinted light between the trees above an open meadow, glimmering with dew. Shifting toward it, I walked into the middle of a lawn which lay there at a thousand feet.

There! Before me! To the south, under the growing blue. Buttressed by dark woodlands: enormous: far gray curtains of rock and ice: leaning against Heaven itself: the Alps!

The Alps

The Alps.

I peered through the morning and I trembled. Before and above me hung sublimely the very veils of Paradise which hide the face of God. From the west and its darkness to the brightened east, for all that my eyes could see, ranged these ragged peaks and their lower folds of woods. There couldn't be enough color in all the world to cover them: they went without. Here and there, affixed like medallions to the folds of these veils, were the villages, the barns and shrines. And amid these I saw the stirrings of men rousing for the day. The tapestry filled my eyes, a weaving of textures and essences and the splendors of morning.

This veil that is the Alps was a rare thing that morning, and magnificent. All before it, in miles of lengthened panels, sat the valley of the river Inn where colored stripes lay which I knew to be fields. The river churned past the town of Zirl below me, in the half-light which lurked in the valley. Green-spattered pastures leaned upward from the riverbed and mixed with the stands of spruce; above these rose the thick silver-greens of black pine. At the timberline, thousands of feet above me, appeared limestone figures of gray riven by veins of ungray. And on the summit, from which the bulk of these mountains depended, an iridescence of ices and vapors shifted in the sun, the morning light suffusing them and endowing them with glory. The vast ensemble of forms drew their strength from beyond this valley, from beyond this world.

The Alps stood sacramentally present to me: physical splendors shedding grace. Tall and wide and grand were they that first morning when I made their acquaintance. The waters and lights waltzed upon their brows, now like a crown, now like a diadem. From the far rim of that valley, their majesty graced one man's soul.

A man must deal with the Alps if he would come to Rome on foot from a far land. They crowd out experiences from the mind. They demand attention. Their rock is inviolable: for though you turn your hands and mind to them, ultimately they stand outside your power to defile.

I was entranced as I made my way down, watching across the valley. With an hour's steps I descended by that still dark and irregular way, *Gasse die Handen Hunderttausend der Wunsch mein*, that way which some call the Street of the Hundred Thousand Hands of My Desire. I tottered into Zirl a little after breakfast time and took away sausages, some fruit yogurt and bread with me over the river by the bridge there. Sitting beside the water to admire the peaks in full light now, I did them reverence in my heart and prayed as I ate my breakfast. And then, with a bow of my head, I rose to make my way toward them, as one makes his way toward a good woman: conscious of my mortality and my faults. I started to march upward to the Brenner Pass.

From the bottom it was a sharp rise of 800 or 900 feet with a gravel roadbed through the spruces and onto a benchland or foreland. The gravel was solid underfoot but steep, and I sweated from my load and the close mist which had slid upon me from the crests. Dante's observation came back to me: in climbing higher one paradoxically relies upon the lower leg. Since this is how Dante did it, this is how it's to be done. I concentrated on each resting lower leg in turn instead of the aching and pulling higher one. Both burned and I told myself there was less oxygen.

When I'd lifted onto this benchland the road leveled off and made toward the southeast beside a cornfield, and then past some scattered houses here, and one or two other houses there. Over one home tucked into a pocket of beech trees was painted a German couplet: "*Sonne klein, aber mein*" ("Not much sun, but it's mine"). The huge Stubai Alps confronted a distant south, with the Kalkskogel near at perhaps 7,500 feet, and nearer still the Nockspitze. My way led to the west of them, not over them. For this I was very,

very thankful. Very thankful.

Bye and bye I tramped into lovely, little Gotzens which is astride a tangle of mountain lanes. Its houses and halls are delightfully trim. They're stained and drawn up on their walls as in the fashion hereabouts. There are barns on its main street with carved and polished hardwood racks upon their faces for drying hay. Gotzens is newer than many little mountain towns though no brighter: that would be pretty difficult.

Stopping at a tavern for lunch to fortify myself with good *bock* beer, I went out again under the sky which brightened after the middle of the afternoon. I strode along a pavement which careered between lush meadows, some of which were mown, with hedges crowding the way. There were short hayricks linked together in threes or fours in the meadows, draped with fresh hay; they looked like grazing green yaks. This road carried me a mile or two toward another little hamlet. Beyond those houses I went to lay down behind a hedge in the sun: but two young lovers were there on a blanket, so I continued on. From there the way made downward for the valley again, so I left it at a rocky wash which scrambled upwards another hundred feet through the scratchy under-growth. This brought me onto a higher southern upland where lay the tiny, sweet village of Mutters.

A devotional crucifix marked a road junction there. I dragged past it after the day of climbing, too tired to find a tavern for supper. I chose my lane outward from Mutters, one that went past a huge vegetable garden. Beside the garden was a rail fence and a bit of grass, and also a fine red bench from which I could see that grand valley leading up to the Brenner Pass from Innsbruck. Here I pitched my tent under a birch.

The light faded and that famous day came to an end. I sat down on the bench there to meditate and to marvel at the gorge of the northern valley, the valley of Innsbruck into which I'd descended at dawn. How many other pilgrims before me had passed here on their way to Rome and the Fisherman. For the longest while I sat in that lovely mountain evening, composing reflections, watching night come into the Tyrol. Ever so slowly, the stars unveiled themselves and assembled against the ebony air.

Mutters Night Sky

I was sitting alone there on that bench above the valley and nudging the ferns with my feet, just keeping company with the night stars, watching the lights below move up the highway toward Italy. There was no moon, but the stars now shone in most of the sky. Lights gleamed from houses on the mountainside; and on the valley floor far below me, the moving lights on the highway resembled comets on a celestial causeway, like caravans of grace. My bench was an outpost against the sky, another Krak de Chevalier where once were found the Knights of the Just and the Knights of Magisterial Grace. And there it occurred to me that, sadly, Moderns are crippled by the example of God. Of all things in which God dwarfs us, surely his extravagance is among the foremost.

The popular attitude toward the stars is telling. Your Modern Alien unacquainted with extravagance in himself is unwilling to believe it of Another. He'll tell you that it's improbable (by which he means wasteful) that Earth alone in all the universe is the only vessel reserved for life. He's intimidated by the thought that the stars are empty and that the whole of the universe is an extravagant, sterile, onyx anchorage in which God has placed with great care this one gleaming tear. But if this is so, if all the remaining universe is lifeless, how awed we should be. What wasteful and unsparing love. Perhaps God has fashioned this whole universe just for our delight and instruction. Like the total gift which spouses make, it's a gift which the Modern Alien hardly understands.

The stars above Mutters are intimations of the wastefulness and the hopefulness of God Who has spent all to win us. Go and sit beneath them of a high summer night, if your soul is troubled. They will restore you.

Beyond Mutters

A glorious morning followed. The night had been cool, almost cold. At first light, I rose in the quiet air, well-chilled with dew. I churned, and stamped the ground, and I blew on my hands, and slapped my arms for warmth. With the blood circulating after some minutes of this, I sat down to watch morning come. Dawn transfigured the valley. The pastel and pearl above began to brighten into blue. In the east, behind a triad of great peaks, the light was growing, reaching onto the ices and stones of the Karwendel range to the south. Behind me, illumined, the Nockspitze received the light above such vapors as shrouded it sides. These shifted upon all sides of the valley, though being vapors they weren't so dense as to veil the tracery of the heights. At this time of year, the alpine huts sprinkled across these mountains would be open. Climbers and wanderers would be sleeping there by night, moving this morning on to the other huts beyond the snow fields.

For upwards of an hour I ate bread and meat, and savored the morning while the chill winds moved about. I wondered at this world where frail human action can effect good and evil; and I wondered at how much there is of both.

I took up my green pack again. Out past the garden I came, past a house or two and then onto a rough mountain lane through a meadow, and into a morning which was lovelier than all telling. For all the world, it seemed that meadow which lies before heaven, and its little road *Weg die Wiese das vor Paradies liegen.*

It had become my habit to keep near villages on this pilgrimage, to keep near my cousins. But I was happy to have that mountain walk under the morning. It was enchanting. Scattered about the summer meadows were ancient log huts ready for this year's hay. The stands of cedars and black firs above me hid many steep thousands of feet. I met no one there as I walked the long, quiet rise of grass.

Poor modern Yourself, with your head full of civic psychology and your heart full of bourgeois dust! Can you possibly know the human happiness of coming out into God's creation of a Tuesday morning in July and stepping off into it whichever way pleases you, with no one to answer to, come what may? No, I suppose not.

A red and black railroad engine pulled a single car up the incline, laboring a little. I saw that I was in a tiny clutch of colored houses with great alpine eaves, Kreith. One of these was remarkable in that it glistened with oil, not paint: a lustrous, soft, tawny patina which let it stand out handsomely. Facing it was a mountain chapel for the Blessed Sacrament, where I stopped to make a visit. From its porch I could see the valley bearing toward the Brenner below the trees.

Beyond Kreith

Beyond Kreith, the lane turned upwards and toward the southwest. There I took my leave of it, delightful though it had been. I descended at an angle through a lower meadow and then through a little copse of larches, on across the railway, and onto a paved road which took me down into the

Tyrolean village of Telfes. There at the ending of the main street was a colorful guesthouse with its mural of hunters in an alpine setting. In front of the mural was a veranda where I sat down at one corner to eat and talk with whomever I might find. You know, I'd become lonely for not finding conversation since Penzberg.

This was my first hot meal since that expensive omelet in Seefeld, and very good it was too. I talked of my adventures with two men who wore *lederhosen* and little tufted hats. They had the courtesy to listen to me instead of volunteering more pedestrian (*sic*) adventures of their own. From them I got the cheapest thing in the world.

Yourself: And what's that?

Myself: Why, advice of course. Here I got advice which is the cheapest thing in the world (a thing to be distinguished carefully from Good Counsel).

Yourself: And what's the dearest thing in the world, since you're so smart?

Myself: Example. What else could it be? There's nothing easier than to give advice, and nothing more difficult than to do good oneself.

As we talked I leaned my chair backwards on two legs against the railing to get a better look at the valley leading up to the Brenner. There with them I leaned and drank beer in the sunlight and considered my life and my many sins which had brought me over the hills toward Rome.

The two men gave me an expectation of the way upwards: of how far it was, and how steep, and where I could stop. I left them. Everywhere there was greenery beneath a wind which brought in the afternoon. Traffic was light on the road; most of it infested the freeway to the west. A rock wall on my right pressed the meadows back against the woods. Downward ran the river Sill beside me.

Steinach

This river Sill is the spine of the village called Matrei, and all the town is gathered along its banks. The place is all done up in mural filligrees of saints or stags and lettering. Steinach, the grander and more prosperous cousin of Matrei, lives up the hill. With mountains to left, right, and front of the town as you approach on foot, it seems hard to believe there's a way out. I climbed into Steinach sluggishly because of the slope and that big meal, weighted down by the afternoon sun. On the gleaming street there I came beneath the statue of a holy man or prelate, quite manly and boldly colored, in a niche across from the church. St. Nepomuk from Furstenfeldbruck came to mind, who shared with this fellow in a hardball piety.

The higher I rose that afternoon the closer the mountains pressed in. More hay fields hoisted from the rail fences, and away eastward onto the Sumpfkopf and the Hohe Warte as well as a dozen lesser peaks of the east. I tried to place these by name as I passed.

Two men stripped to the waist were haying an upturned meadow where I came round a bend in the road. We saluted. The older one was pushing a motorized swather on two wheels. His blond younger mate was higher up the slope, taking the measure of the mountain with the slow rhythmic whisper of a hand scythe so that the hillside was corrugated where he'd climbed. The cut hay scented the air which had settled into those narrows. There was a great harvest of hay laying beneath them, for it was late afternoon and they had been cutting many hours.

The Sill and the road now began to jostle one another in the press between the steeps, the stream first on my left, then burrowing to my right. Its liquid effects of pearl-green and white swirled among the rocks of the stream bed. But the two behaved themselves well enough to allow me to get upwards. I didn't know how near the Pass I was: the slopes and the trees allowed no view of any distance. I toyed with the idea of pressing on into Italy that night. But it was evening now and my pocket was miraculously choked with schillings. (I've already told you how I'd miscalculated the exchange ratio all across Austria.)

Pension Rose

Providentially I didn't press on. Instead I halted in Gries, very tired, and came to the Pension Rose, which is one of the sanctuaries provided for us in this world. It was old and worn, like our homes, and inviting. The dining room was the heart of that house. Perhaps thirty happy souls could be served in it. There was a worn slat floor and wood walls, with ceiling panels handpainted in floral detail. The small corner bar was painted too. All the chairs were carved and stenciled. They were placed at tables which were draped with white linens. Only the green ceramic stove against one wall was other than wood. What a warm and human place that dining room was.

There I found a good innkeeper, and his gracious daughter who made a little fuss over me. I fell in love with her.

She wasn't pretty in the superficial way of some women, but she was attractive, very feminine and pleasant to be near, and easy on the eye. Her manner was quiet, even reverent as she seated each of her guests at evening in that old room. Her face was broad and round, and framed by dark hair falling lightly to her shoulders. When she addressed me her voice was full and soft, and low in a lovely way for a woman. She was fashioned more of flesh than bone, and in her eyes there was no guile. While serving my soup, this woman's fragrant hair lightly passed upon the top of my own. And from that moment she has had a friend.

Several times she found me studying her from across the room where she sat sewing beneath the corner crucifix. Each time she smiled or roused herself to ask if she might serve me further. I never wished as hard for fluency in another tongue as I did that evening. But there was little use in wishing. I had no way of knowing whether I was mistaking simple courtesy for a woman's affection. And it's so important to know.

By ten o'clock the other guests had gone and the

kitchen was closed. I crossed bashfully and told her good
night. She questioned me carefully about my purpose and my
pack, but I knotted up (as can happen when one tries to talk
with a good woman). I couldn't find my words. Ashamed of
my mumbling, I paid her and said another good night, and
then I climbed within that good house to my room.

She was a good woman, that young woman in Gries. If
the Blessed are as gracious as she, I'll be happy to join them.

In the morning after a profound mountain sleep I went
down early to breakfast, but the woman was not there. I
nearly despaired. I ate slowly in sorrow, paid my fare, and
then I left for Rome. The road had a new name for me, as so
often before, because of the good young woman: *Gasse fur
die Badewanne freimachen das Mitleid*, the Street of the
Loosening Bath of Mercy.

Within minutes I was at the border plaza, where I came
up against Authority. On the Italian side I stood search: my
pack was rummaged and I came near to arrest when my vi-
tamins and salt tablets were discovered. In my malodorous
walking clothes, with so many days of beard from ear to sun-
tanned ear, my cap ringed with salt, my maps and papers
jammed every which way into my shirt, I looked like any
other disreputable vagrant. The Italian sergeant, who wore
his cap indoors as a mark of authority, demanded to see my
money while the guard examined my passport. I think it was
the map of my route as much as my explanation which per-
suaded them. I boasted in *lingua franca* of my pilgrimage and
of the route of my brave march—this because I thought I
was winning with them. The sergeant relented. He took my

passport from the guard and stamped it with a vigorous
pound.

Yourself: Isn't that *lingua franca* something like Es-
peranto? Sort of?

Myself: I wouldn't know. All I know is that it worked.

I paused on the plaza there, dedicating myself with
thanks and supplication. Then, drawing a deep breath
through a grin, I stepped off soundly into Italy.

Brenner Pass

Triumphantly I swung down off the Brenner, composing
prose celebrations of the day. How proud of myself I was
that morning. Hadn't I pushed manfully across all Franconia,
slain the ancient Danube, then taken Bavaria at a rush and
left it for dead in my wake? Hadn't I bested at a run all those

holy terrors, the Prealps, then jumped the Inn by cunning? And hadn't I stormed the face of the Alps themselves with vigor, taking Italy bare-handed by virtue of my manliness?

I say plainly that I had one glorious day.

Presumption and Despair are twin evils and the Faith admonishes against either one. There was no danger to me of Despair that morning. But I'm not so sure about the Presumption. It was an allure. May God grant us all a very close brush with Presumption.

Below the Pass is the rich valley of the Adige. Its color pulled me into itself. To the west and away rises the steep Eisack range: Steinjoch, Kreuzjoch, and Geierskragen magnificent at 2,200 meters, more of the frontier. Their brethren stand to the east at 2,500 meters. Between them passes the Isarco, descending. Blue spruces have spilled off the heights and stand on the weathered lower edges, baring red rock gashes about them. Waterfalls, multiple and abrupt, slide downward in free-falling cataracts from the glaciers, into and then through the timber walls of the valley, and across the bright array of narrow meadows or vineyards or orchards, and so into the river. Lower into this valley I came with the day.

The road twisted left and right time and again, weaving downward between the slopes. I was surprised to still be facing forward when I came into Vipiteno which the Germans call by its alias of Sterzing. It's a decorous town at the meeting of the Isarco valley with that lesser one of the Ridanna.

If you come down to Vipiteno on a Saturday afternoon in the heat of the summer and you turn in to the *centro*, you'll find the good life. Boys are chatting up the pretty young shop girls who wear summer dresses of muslin. Old couples murmur approvals and conversation over their coffees beneath the street-side umbrellas. Shoppers stroll the cobblestones beneath the bay windows. The whole street sits in the shade of tall shop buildings. The colors are subtler and more elegant for the shade: all the grays, and the reds and ochres, the greens and even the garish tones of the umbrellas—all are muted by the shade. The smells of coffee and leather enlace with those of wine or picked fruit. The whole aspect of the street is that of the want of haste. It's hard not to regret a life spent away from Vipiteno on a Saturday afternoon in the Italian summer.

Vipiteno

Before you hear the words of the visitors in town you can tell their languages: by their cadences and their keys, and by their timbre. British is sing song and swollen of tongue: it's slow. German is abrupt and rather clipped, harsh, with a crisp authority that irritates. Italian—ah Italian is the elegant air: varied, fluid and sculpted: Italian, so suited to the ladies' needs.

Beyond town is a valley plaza a mile or more across. To one side of the valley sits a castle on its forehill. There my river turned plainly toward Rome, working its way to the east around the Sarntaler Alps. The whole valley was dotted with chapels and churches and shrines. It was awash in the Faith. Paul Verlaine evoked such a valley road in a single verse: "Oh, the highways of the Middle Ages, lined with chapels and gallows."

It began to rain a little at day's end. Stopping at a white inn beyond Vipiteno where the valley levels out, an inn behind a huge and distinguished willow, I was disappointed for a room. The little girl in the yard there (about five I think) told me she knew there was no room but she brought out her mother anyway who told me the same thing. The little girl stole her mother's thunder by volunteering politely the directions to another place further down the valley. The mother, with her arms folded, smiled at her daughter and nodded agreement. I left. A mile further on I found a lane beside Campo del Trens and shuffled up it to a whitewashed farmhouse which serves as an inn there.

The farmer himself greeted me quizzically in the barnyard and pleaded ignorance. "I don't know if there is a room left tonight. We were filled last night but some of the guests may be leaving." He left his work in the milk barn and, with a farm friend, invited me into the house while the wife was sent for. Directly, he produced schnaps there in the kitchen, pouring a measure for each of the three of us.

"*Salute*," the farmer toasted.

"Up the long ladder and down the short rope; etcetera." I fired mine back, while they sippped slowly and remarked between them about my ignorant haste with drink.

"Where are you coming from? More importantly, where

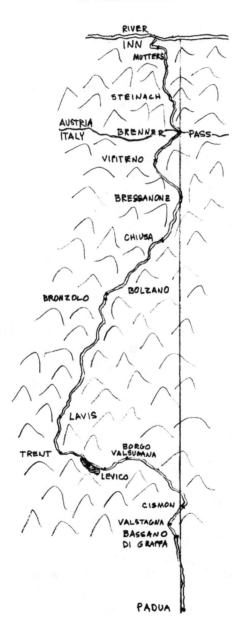

are you going?" the farmer asked me in German.

"I'm coming from beyond Nurnberg and I'm on my way to Rome. I'm a pilgrim. You probably don't get many like me in here."

"Well how much distance have you walked to here?" he asked.

"The whole way: over three hundred miles now. Three hundred down, four hundred to go," I tossed off. It amazed me as I said it.

With nods and a pursing of the lips they both drank the rest of their schnaps. The wife appeared about then and looked around the room. I sat up straight, while the schnaps and both men vanished. She apologized that there was only one room left, a double room at full price. (She was a solid businesswoman.) With lightning wit I countered that I would sleep for two (she thought this very clever of me), and the bargain was struck.

There was no evening meal given at the farmhouse so I hobbled up the gravel trail to the center of Campo del Trens where I found the inn marked by the postal horn. Such places named for the old post routes are usually a good bet in Europe. It so happened that evening that the serving girl was more interested in her young friends than in me. It took extra long for me to get a simple cordon bleu with wine and bread.

That night I did as I had told the house mistress: I slept for two.

In the morning there was a huge breakfast of coffee with milk (a full pitcher of each), a basket of rolls, and a pot of currant jam. I took my cue from two couples who had also spent the night there: I stuffed myself and left nothing but wicker and pottery and the flatware on the table linen. And then I paid up. This first Italian duty was a happy surprise, because the farmer charged me only the price of a single bed.

"But the agreement with your wife was that I would pay double," I warned him.

"She'll get over it," was his sly reply. "You have a long way to go yet."

Belvư Vipitano

"Done."

My first day in Italy was all downhill. The valley of the Isarco, the green and whitewater Isarco, is narrow. It is very deep country. And there's a wind which freshens the land along the river at morning. The semi-forested hills here are abrupt. When the sunlight shines it brightens the rock upon the hills, but not the trees. The flat of the valley, which is not wide here, is under an emerald brome; and upon this grass are seen, from time to time, the small pearlescent flocks minded by shepherds. Lizards scoot along the roadside. These lizards were something new on the Italian side of the Pass, as were the prickly hedgehogs which had been flattened to the pavement.

Which reminds me of a fine little book by Isaiah Berlin I'd like to recommend, *The Hedgehog and the Fox*; but let's not get into that. Instead let's just think about hedgehogs for a minute. In Europe hedgehogs milk cows, as those who should know will verify. Hedgehogs raid apple orchards too, and carry off little apples on the spines of their back, but what they do with them is anybody's guess. Maybe they carry them as tribute to foxes, because foxes otherwise will seek out the little hedgehogs and roll them down to a place where there is water. There the hedgehogs open up from their defensive ball rather than drown; and that is the end of the hedgehog. But this too reminds me of Isaiah Berlin's book, and as I say, let's not get into that.

As you walk the Isarco in July the heat will collect over you. But if you're happy afoot you'll pay it no mind. Satisfaction will gather in you as the momentum draws you downward. For you'll have passed the greatest barrier to Rome. You'll be almost half way to Rome and still going strong. Under the tall Italian morning you'll be moving downward.

I divided the miles remaining to me into 30 mile days, 16 hour days, and other concoctions of vanity. Within days, not weeks, I fancied myself triumphantly entering the walls of Rome, throngs cheering me on, television cameras packed into a van driven before me, with myself gesturing magnanimously to the crowd with open hands in the fashion of a lord.

If you ask me, I'd become a bit much. What do you think?

Yourself: Well, I wasn't going to bring it up; but now that you mention it, yes, I think you had, just a bit.

Myself: Maybe I'd lost the thing called hilarity. In the saner ages gone before us folks possessed *hilaritas.* They remembered that since the Fall every effort of life is attended by imperfection—by a troubling—and so each requires the leaven of mirth. But I, remembering the solemnity of my purpose—I had forgotten the Fall. It's the plainest fact in all the world, the Fall. I'd forgotten it. Within hours it would be remembered to me.

Absorbed with myself I swaggered ahead and downward, my hands in my pockets, little more than noticing the valley all about me. Low walls of fitted rock lined a country lane which I passed above Mittewald (not Mittenwald, should any pedant still be lurking).

Fortezza

Below Fortezza stood its namesake fortress athwart the road: massive cut planes of boulders vaulting from the mountain onto a bed of rock beyond a greenwater lake. Here the water ran between two woods. The fine vineyards of Italy appeared to one side, pegged onto the hillsides above the bright villages, with the chain they call Sarntaler ranged beyond them to the west. Above all of this hung a polished sun which punished me with its bright heat.

Sitting on a mound of dried concrete I drank a whole litre of cola to quench my thirst, but it only made things worse. I rounded a bend and looked out over Bressanone less than an hour's walk beyond. Being reluctant to deal with a city yet, I went into a little meadow at hand and sat under a solitary white poplar spreading just above a stream. I lowered my feet into the water and leaned back. The water was cold. Since drinking the cola, I had nothing with me to slake my thirst. I bent to drink from the stream, and filled my belly with handfuls of the cold water until I could drink no more.

Therein I founded my ruin.

With my feet cooler after the bath, I strolled through the next hour of heat into Bressanone, where the valley widens: Bressanone, with its name like the speaking of cellos. It's filled with symphonies of luxuriant oaks which shade its boulevards and the houses and gates of its rich men. These oaks stand in regular, clipped rows like staves of plainchant. I passed a squad of soldiers, infantrymen by their collar brass, in front of their garrison. Conjecturing among themselves about my pack and boots, they nodded me their recognition, and I made my return.

I entered a news shop just beyond the garrison to buy better maps of the Dolomites. Pulling out my own worn map as an illustration of what I wanted, I showed the old woman my line of march to Rome and the notes scribbled along that line so far. Then, without the least provocation, I began the history of my march, pointing out to her places where I'd enjoyed adventures. Maybe the old woman was envious of my satisfaction and good humor; she only looked at me in a most peculiar way, and provided me neither maps nor help. I've thought since then that she may have put the evil eye on me— the *mal occhio*—because I suffered a calamity only miles beyond her shop. But on that day I just folded up my map and passed good naturedly through the beaded curtain into the street.

The heat, as I've said, was fierce, noticeably hotter than it had been in Austria. Those next miles were a struggle downward into swells of heat and hot July wind. There was little shade along the road for many miles. I grew aware of the Italian sun's power.

I began to suffer. Keeping to the road, I shambled ahead feeling very queer in the head, and weak. But pressing on I made Chiusa by suppertime. Clomping onto that timber bridge which crosses the Isarco above town, I came around the back side and along the lush river promenade to where I found a shady patch of ground to lay upon. A little ways from me was a new restaurant below that castle which commands from the sheer cliffs. There were patrons aplenty and I tried to persuade myself to eat. But I was now feeling puny, whether sick or merely tired I didn't know. And so while it

Chiusa at dusk

was still evening and light out, I lay down.

Between the ague which now gripped me and that cold night which followed, I tossed fitfully for hours. Not until after midnight could I sleep.

It was late morning before I awoke from a short sleep, and crept into Chiusa town. I wasted an hour in the shops, hoping for pity or human consolation (but no one talked to me) before I forced myself onto the road south.

Already I was tired, immensely tired. The collective effort of the past two weeks assembled in my mind and pressed down my spirit. I began to know that I was ill: feverish, aching, parched, and nauseous. I pushed my way along the road. Something was wrong. I was fearful. Was it merely Summer Complaint? My mind climbed backward toward Bressanone and the mountain water. Had it been tainted? Had I poisoned myself by a hasty drink? I only knew that I was dis-eased and shuffling, creeping beneath a sun which crippled me.

A German family in their Mercedes offered me a lift but I fought the temptation and refused. I was on pilgrimage. Close by, I dragged into a tavern. By now I was in a swoon. For two hours I waited on the heat and tried to eat and drink. It was no use. I slumped there in a chair under a grape arbor. The old woman grew uneasy and sent me out, sometime after one in the hot part of the day.

I followed the greenwater Isarco downward past the castles, beyond dead buildings in places, past the shapeless hamlets until it entered that gorge which presses in upon all things that stray there, including the mind. I moved by reflexes for another two or three hours until, drained of strength, I made Bolzano late in the day. My eye caught almost nothing of the town except that I saw no inns. I spent another hopeless hour slumped on a weathered bench on a boulevard, beside a cantaloupe vendor. He wore an undershirt and a porkpie hat, and he called out to passersby far too often. When I thought I'd fall asleep on that bench I stood up giddily and wandered on along the boulevard. The sun died a violent death at the hands of sharpened bloody clouds. Onward I slouched: crumpled, bent, worn.

An innkeeper refused me because his house was filled. Perhaps a half hour later I found a small hostel across from an orchard where I was admitted with suspicion only after producing money. It was a mere closet I was given there, with no windows to the outside and only a colored glass onto the hallway. Inside, on that tiny bed, I grew frightened. I believed myself alone, which is the very worst thing ever to think.

The whole night was a farrago of fevers and deliriums, of prayers for mercy. I slept very little and rested not at all. At morning I was drained.

I was in danger and knew it as I staggered out from the stale air of that closet toward Rome at midmorning. As it says in Deuteronomy, "the heavens above me were brass and the earth beneath me iron." Hearing and taste and smell were gone from me. I saw as if I were on stilts. The heat pained my face and neck and my arms. I didn't so much walk as shift the flats of my feet over the road. My knees no longer bent. I came ahead like a manikin. Little was left of my reason. Barely enough of my will remained to bring me forward. Pity me: I was a pillar of fire, and a column of prayer.

Agony gnawed my mind. Horrible fears invested my spirit. My pilgrimage was in certain peril. I cursed that drink of water above Bressanone.

Tottering now, I chose desperate little goals along the roadside: that driveway ahead; that second road marker ahead; the largest shade tree to the left. Not Rome any longer but little ten yard marches became my marks. My head and arms drooped, my eyes were fixed just beyond my feet. Sweat raced down my face and chest. Dozens of times I forced myself forward to another mark. Twice cars honked me from the road where I'd wandered.

At one mark which was a clot of bushes, I stumbled sideways into the weeds, rolling onto a large flat rock there. My chest heaved, my blood raced. There was no part of me that didn't ache. Trying to rise silently, I got to one elbow but sank again onto my pack.

Cars hurried past on the road, sending blasts of July air under the bushes where I lay. I slipped my pack, I strained and pressed, but I couldn't rise. I prayed, but I couldn't rise. I deceived myself, but I could not rise from that rock.

In those hot weeds beside the road to Rome, I lay back and despaired. Something great had defeated me.

I quit.

In midafternoon the stifling heat brought me to and goaded me out from under that brush. A mile or so on I found Bronzolo. Somehow I negotiated a ticket, somehow I lasted the wait for an ugly brown train. Northward I rode, only so much limp baggage: back up the long alpine valley, back over the high Brenner, across Austria, then back across the length of Bavaria to Schesslitz. From there the fevers drove me sickened, back from that lovely smile of Europe, and across the sea, back onto the prairie.

There is only one human thing worth wanting: and that is being home. It is the one thing that matters to the heart of a man.

Bronzolo Station

They say that God chastens those he would grace. I can believe that. To the pilgrim who is to be graced, this chastening may be his banishment from home, his living the life of an exile. For they say that our home is not of this world, those who should know. It may be so.

I have been told, "You don't know when to quit. That's the trouble with you: you don't know when to quit. Don't be so obstinate. Be realistic. You'll get over your disappointment; you'll see. Time heals all hurts. It's nonsense to be so serious about such a trifle as a failed pilgrimage." This is what I've been told.

Yet others have said it is not so. Ysè, the woman who is not happiness but is in the place of happiness, once spoke at the break of noon.

'Be annealed by your failure and keep faith as best you can. A man should have a backbone in him. Accept your penance; you might well deserve worse than this. Keep faith and persevere in your heart. By all means persevere. God often delays without denying. Be faithful. You'll see: God is known for His mercy.'

Failure and sorrow and, at last, death are the true human adventures, it is said. But there is another; there is waiting. For the best we can do in our waiting is to hope to be called nearer, to hope to be called home. That's the best we can do. And that too is an adventure. Waiting too is an adventure. For the pilgrim.

I have been told, "It's hopeless. Nothing more can be done. You did your best and no one can do any more than that. It's hopeless now. Put your failure behind you. What else can be done by a man but do without? It's all quite impossible now, really."

Yet Madame Gervaise, cloistered in a convent in Loraine, once spoke from the portico of the mystery of the second virtue:

'If there weren't hope, there would be nothing at all in this old world. Nothing at all. Hope is our anchor. Only through hope will you gain the hoped-for. It is never wrong to hope, never too late to hope. Lazarus the good friend of God was already four days in his tomb when he was called near.'

I am told that from great evil, very great good comes. That may be. But I cannot see the help given to any human heart by exile and loneliness, by banishment from home. I really can't. A man who has made ready to celebrate homecoming, who has prepared himself to receive the twin chrisms of Visitation and Welcome, but finds exile instead, suffers horribly. And even though his love—which is the best thing in him—remains firm, still he finds himself carried farther and farther from his home by the wash of time. And I doubt that good is done by it all. But they say that very great good can come of this.

"You're wasting your time over this pilgrimage," I am told. "Be sensible. Be reasonable. Detach from all this. Save yourself a lot of unhappiness. Stop wasting your time. Give it up. Forget this pilgrimage. Don't talk any more foolishness."

Yet Clotilde, the woman who was poor, once spoke from the slum streets of Paris where she knelt before a little child:

'God blesses with a cross. He is a priest and the cross is His way. Remember that. Remain constant in your heart. Always. Do not yield, but rather endure. Whoever remains faithful to the end in His love will be saved.'

I have been told that virtues, to be virtues, must be lived. And a quest, to be a quest, must be undertaken. Talking and regretting are not the way; doing is the way. If a man would come home, then at least once in his life he must rise onto his own two legs and do what he can for himself. This is a hard saying. But this is what I've been told.

Dorothy Day, beloved by Our Lord, once spoke from a house of hospitality where she lived, on pilgrimage:

'Work and pray. These are the two things you must do to be a pilgrim or a saint. The rest is up to God. The heart of all life is prayer. Celebrate your prayer. If you can do that much, if you can work and pray, you can become a pilgrim or a saint. Begin now. + In the name of the Father, and of the Son, and of the Holy Spirit. Amen.'

Those hundreds of miles and those long painful days afoot had worn heavily upon me. But that long exile which followed nearly wore me out.

As long as we have our souls must we be faithful. And we have our souls forever.

One Saturday evening one May I climbed down with my pack from a chocolate brown coach, and stood again in front of the station in Bronzolo. The custard and drab facade was as hateful to me that evening as it had been too many seasons before when it marked the tomb of my effort. Studied closely by a local *carabiniere* in his white bandolier, I paced once around the station confidently, studying it while I remembered my defeat here. I turned my back on it and crossed slowly to a restaurant behind that garden on the alley. In there I feasted on veal and bread and a tall pilsen. As I ate I remembered, and composed myself to begin again.

I wouldn't be hurried in Bronzolo that May evening. Not this time. I would be in command of myself. I would methodically rechristen my purpose. "This is the site of my ruin," I said to myself. "God be pleased, may the good people between here and Rome send me along until I finish."

Outside on the dusty street, beside the orchard and the birds, I lifted that rumpled old green pack onto my shoulders again by the strength of my own two arms, and I set my worn blue cap again upon my head. I hammered my tall pine staff one time loudly upon the ground as an announcement. And then I walked off once more into Italy, toward Rome. My pilgrimage was restored.

On either side of the street I saw the little lanes leading off past the houses and shops of the town. An old peasant with a worn and chiseled face above his open shirt greeted me with puzzlement that evening in the town, and then walked quietly beside me while I crowed. At a fork in the road just beyond the town was a bench under a big poplar, and on the bench sat a young couple. The old man chuckled at the lovers and pointed me to the east of them. There I left him, and swung on down the road under the Dolomites and the rosy dusk.

Swallows were still busy in the apple orchards, while the people of this valley were inside at supper. The Italian

Lane in Bronzolo

evening decanted its watercolor over the old gashes in my heart: a magenta balm proper to healings as to enchanted evenings.

Now, after so long, I was shed of Bronzolo. I tried to pay attention to the mountains and fields, but I was looking inward a great deal, laughing, cheering myself on. My happiness was pure and deep, like a lamb standing among lilies. I walked purposefully. For those first dusky miles I made a great flourish: the first evening of any importance for me in months. The forms and airs, the colors of the valley returned to me in *pentimento*. (Pentimento: the artist repents.) Even the Fiats rushing along the road couldn't temper my happiness. So I came slowly onward toward Aura some three hours beyond.

The vast fields in the west end of Heaven were ablaze, sending up smokes and grays which darkened the curve of the sky and then lay out above all the land ahead. The sky had brought on the night by the time I made Aura, a little footsore. I missed the painted sign to a campground, so I had to make a hasty search while a rumble set up somewhere in the darkness above. A gravel lane led me past a walled eighteenth century villa and its large hall, where a great company of revelers were singing and carrying on in the yellow light. Catholics most likely. Beyond the villa and to the right, I found a little square, and beside the square a white inn, barely marked. A kind young woman there charged me dearly for a room and set beer before me on a wet pine table to the right of the door.

I was excited by my return to the road and not able to sleep, so I considered how to while away the last of the evening without walking. The night outside was calm, and lit by a quarter moon whose two horns grazed slowly higher and deeper into the sky. I went out with my beer, attracted to the dark and empty square beside the inn, and I sat down on the low wall of a stone trough that was there. It was running full to the rim with cool water into which I dipped my hand, water fallen from a spigot. So too the square was filled with the little sound of the water's advent, provided in that way with a murmuring presence apart from that of the villagers now gone to their homes. With feet of starlight, the water alighted from the mountain, and entered the square with the tenderness of a suitor, unaccompanied, breaking silence in endearments, *pianissimo*, flowing deeply then into the dark trough and causing song to lift like a meditation onto the night airs. Silence coupled itself to this calm serenade of the people: a gentle evensong amid the niello and starlight, a tender nocturne mixing in ensemble the voices of water and stone. The song seemed that of a returning lover's greeting: "Don't be afraid. It is I. I've come back to you."

The clock atop the church tower across from me sounded ten. An old dog barked in the distance. A woman, with her arms crossed and a sweater draped over her shoulders against the air, hurried past me in the dark, and turned up a bent street toward the mountain. Yellow light from an upper window of the inn brushed the edge of the paving stones in the square.

Sitting upon that ledge I grew content under the influence of the night. I thanked God for that water flowing down from above, fragrant and cool and given voice, constant like our Faith, sustaining the people of this valley. Only real water sings like that in the night. Only a real woman is worth every effort. Only a real pilgrimage leads a man into and out of the valleys. And only the Faith sends water into our parched souls.

Knowing that all this was no fantasy but rather a sacrament, a great favor preserved to me for my return, I went in to sleep once again as a pilgrim, leaving the low wall of a stone trough that was there. It was running full to the rim with cool water into which I'd dipped my hand, water fallen from a spigot. The stones of the square were mindful of the sound of the water's advent, provided in that way with a murmuring presence apart from that of the villagers and of a solitary footman, all gone to their homes.

That night a fierce storm appeared. The rain hurtled down and beat against the house and its windows so that I wakened, on and off.

At daybreak the church bells sounded. It was Sunday. By the time I dressed I was late for first Mass (the one in German), coming in late at the consecration. I waited for the next Mass (the one in Italian: the Faith speaks every tongue) before I was off.

I like these Italians. They suit my temperament more than the Germans. They're used to the heat and to level ground in places, just like I am. They're so very long of the Faith that they're a little reckless with it. But they're good people and they come back to it when there's trouble.

Here in the Dolomites the people are part Austrian and part Italian. The Austrian in them is mad for bright paint. I remembered this while looking at the sharp colors and the painted filligree which clambered over the walls of the houses, public and private. The ways of the Germans and Austrians returned now to me. Beyond the printed signs and the painted shops and walls, I came out into a valley between the great heaps of the Dolomites where the western rock was gilded with sunlight. Below, where I walked, the valley was veiled with a cool gauze which was good for walking all morning.

Beyond aura

The maker of the Dolomites must have been in a hurry. Whether archangel or mountain god, he seems to have used a broadaxe to rough-out their shape and then gone on—and a blunt axe at that. Split rock faces mark the transformation from the lower to the higher slopes of trees. It was these rocks which the sun gilded in places. Below them, on the valley floor, sat the villages and their orchards.

At the midday halt it began to rain lightly. Here and there I took a lane to cut the angle of the turning broadway, but I kept to the edge of the highway mostly, as it curved grandly past the orchards and the dense vineyards. People honked and waved as they roared past (most of them in good cheer) but none gave me money: talk is cheap. A multi-colored swarm of cyclists pedalled past me, raising a great mist on the asphalt. Straining and sweating, bent so low, they clogged the road with churning legs and spray, escorted fore and aft by police sedans. You'd have thought they were walking and not riding from the strain showing in their faces. It took a good twenty minutes for all three hundred of them to go by.

I stopped for food in a roadside bar out of the rain, though there were only chocolates and ice cream at that hour. Soon I left. It began to rain again for the fifth time that day and the easy-to-reach mark of Lavis now grew more distant. I was footsore because, as so long ago, I hadn't trained for my walk. So I just squatted under an awning and calculated the time and distance to Trent, some miles beyond. Given that it was about four in the afternoon, I stood and set out over the river Aviso by a bridge which seemed to be of the same drab cloth as the river: the both of them filled brimful with turgid, silver water. It was still like that, with water falling and running all about me, when I came down the last of the highway into Trent, an hour later.

When I could see the steeple through the clouds I broke out into "76 Trombones" and "Consider Yourself At

Home," two great tunes for singing *fortissimo* and for per-
cussion with the staff. There on the outskirts of Trent I created a minor pageant for myself, singing, gesturing, stepping,
and pounding, though I waited for the traffic to thin out before twirling my staff (drummajor-wise, as the journalist
said).

The cathedral of Trent is a fortress. It's all business. Inside it is dark and somber and plain. Without, it's composed:
weathered: unmoved. Here a battle was fought for the unity
of Christendom. And here, by the bishops in council, the battle was saved. You can see where chunks of limestone have
fallen from the cathedral ramparts, but the cathedral remains, evidence of the vivacity and resolve of our Faith.

Trent served its turn well; but that was all another time.
The new glory of the Faith is the Second Vatican Council.
What a motherload of grace it has proven to be. Apart from
the misuse that Aliens have put it to, the Council has caused
beautiful transfigurations of this ancient Faith of ours.

Catholicism now possesses a renewed ability to sanctify the world, and to complete the evangelization of mankind that was thwarted five hundred years ago. In all of Modernity, there is no other sufficient opponent of the manifold forms of tyranny and despair available save the Faith: not politics for sure, nor law, not psychology certainly, not journalism, not theatre nor music, nor commerce. Not anything but Christianity: articulate, happy, prayerful Christianity. However much the Aliens attempt to seduce us into lesser efforts than evangelization, or treat Vatican II as an Anti-Council, a Council of the Total Critique, the Council Fathers contradict them. Every earnest Christian should be proud of this Council, and find in it that continuing intervention of the Divine which is our patrimony.

In the morning there was more soft Italian rain. I

above Trent

threaded my way eastward through the wet city. I knew I was now west of the line to Rome by twenty miles. When I had been shuffling above Bronzolo in delirium, I'd taken the main road, which didn't follow the line. It was time I corrected my march. I came past the cathedral, the flesh of my wet feet crumbling, out to the gardens east and onto that wet road which writhes upon the mountains, the mountains where the valley Valsugana lies. It was a climb of perhaps a thousand feet first crack out of the box that morning, and it knocked the starch right out of me. That road was a widow-maker.

At a fork in the road I bore to the right atop the box-end of a canyon. From there I crossed diagonally with the road to the canyon's upper side. The road hung atop hundred foot pilons, and curved in a gentle arc, which ignored the stream beneath it, and disregarded too that lake which is somewhere in the hills above.

Only the slopes at hand were visible through the mists. I climbed higher through the drizzle, and then into a series of dark tunnels bored through the hills which I used rather than walk around. The tunnels were black and long and they dripped with waters. Each was littered with rotten roadside trash. And when trucks passed each was full of noise. Such tunnels must be based on a design from Hell: a pure oppression of the spirit, a most unnatural place.

Beyond a midmorning town of no consequence which was up there somewhere, a blue road sign pointed upwards to Levico. My map showed that I should carry on along the floor between the mountains and beside a lake, but I doubted and turned upward at the sign. Well. After less than a mile I found I had to be part billy goat to walk that road. Now, I'm in no way part billy goat, and I haven't a single ancestor with the cloven hoof. So I backtracked and took to the low road beside lake Caldonazzo, a broad water lying all in a calm, and then past the villages which sit on its further shore.

It was the only thing thereabouts which was horizontal, that lake: wide and gray and slick and bereft of light under the overcast. There were vineyards behind me, but I was intent upon the water and the gray haze which softened the rock faces beyond. As I walked I shared the way with heavy traffic and diesel fumes. Slowly I came up from the lake's tip to Levico on its mountainside. The restaurants and the bars were closed because it was still before the resort season. But in a hotel there the girl gave me beer, though she couldn't find anything for me to eat. Because nothing was doing, I came along the streets and past the church on its plaza perch, past the shuttered hotels and shops, and down onto the little road which skips across the hay fields of the valley Valsugana.

Lake Caldonazzo

Yourself: Same old one and two, huh? Same old open road?

Myself: Exactly. Same old open road.

My feet were sore but my legs were aching more. I was dealing with fresh pain like that I'd suffered beyond Schesslitz earlier. "Soon," I reminded myself, "my feet will toughen. I'll hit my stride." I took heart. But it was still a hobble which took me through the long mountain rains of that afternoon. To look at me wrapped in my poncho and poking ahead, you would have thought me not long for it. You'd have been wrong.

To boost my spirits I sang a long song damning English recruitment in Ireland, "Arthur McBride and the Sergeant;" I sang it three or four times out there in the countryside. It recalls an encounter by Arthur McBride and his cousin, with the recruiting sergeant and a little drummer, beside the sea on a Christmas morning in Ireland. Arthur and his cousin get the better of it.

Levico, I found, was the crest of my crossover march through the Valsugana back to the direct line for Rome again. From there the road was an easy rolling downward way through the high meadows which lead you on toward Padua.

Now by a beaten way, then by a lane, here by a road, I settled into the floor of the Valsugana at a pace which taxed but didn't break me. Above, an overcast waited. At times the sun would burn through and set fire to the edges of the clouds, which framed in brilliant whites a plate of pure blue beyond. And then all would be hidden again by another overcast.

The Brenta river was busying itself downward, working its noisy white and gray way among the rocks. Bye and bye I drew beneath a lush oak promenade, and at the end found Borgo Valsugana. It's cheery and well-ordered, and it's charmed by the sweep of the river all in a cradle there. Near the river, there is a grocer's shop front of polished woods and brass. And inside the shop is a good woman of courtesy.

You'll know her by the chignon which she makes of her hair and too by the knitting at which she works behind the counter. I bought canned pork from her and a bottle of fruit juice (most of it on her recommendation). She gave me encouragement in our common *lingua franca*. She smiled at me and let me repack my belongings on the cool shop floor. To thank her, I showed her my maps with the lengthening column of notes beside the single line upon it. I told her of one or two of my adventures, but she had little interest in them. Her mind was in commerce, and courtesy, and her knitting of course. As I left, she recited a litany of the distances to the little towns before Padua. It was her way of helping me.

My good spirits lasted only for a couple of miles, until I sat down beside a bridge for lunch. There I blundered onto an ant nest six feet across, one that looked like barren ground. I sat down there. Dozens of ants quickly proved that it wasn't what it seemed. I leaped up and scratched. I rubbed and swore while I bolted down a can of pork. And that's when my good spirits left me: when I sat on that ant nest at lunch.

The mountains pressed in closely beyond Borgo, so that the road had to shift and fetch for room more than before. It made for Ospedaletto, named because of the hospital there I didn't see. I take their word for it that it's there though.

Yourself: Not very scientific that, taking their word for it.

Myself: Don't believe everything you're told about science. There were signs all along that road used by thousands of Italians. And the signs all told that distance to the hospital. The proof was sufficient. Dr. Johnson supports me in this.

Yourself: Please! No more Dr. Johnson.

Myself: Alright then.

I was past Ospedaletto in no time (it sits right beside the road), because it's tiny. On the far side of town I stopped short. I heard behind me the ringing of the village church bell. My immediate hope was to get Mass, yet it was midday and too late for Mass. Only when the bells quit ringing did it come back to me: the Angelus.

I was delighted! I said the Angelus there where I stood beside the road. I did well to do so. On the prairie we don't have that intimate daily visitation with the Faith which comes in the Angelus. We do without, and we are the poorer for it. We have Justice Black's notorious Wall of Separation between church and state, the ass! To find the Faith so readily at hand in each common day is a pure benediction for us.

The Valsugana

The premier minds and hearts of every age grapple with the Incarnation.

For two millenia, since Our Lord first sent Peter out into deep water, we've steered by a golden dove with five wounds, wounds which bleed light. We've sailed past tens of failed religions and emperors: past Arians, Huns, and Hussites, Mongols; past Cathars, and Nazis, and Manichaeans, Incas, Moors; on past the Druids, the Romans, the Prussians, the Elizabethans, and the Hapsburgs; past the Anabaptists, and the Goths . . . Past them all.

The Incarnation causes and sustains what sanity and clarity is found these days among men. DeGaulle, Irishman de Valera, de Gasperi of Italy, and Adenauer, the founders of four ordered nations were sons of the Church. So is Lech Walesa whose foundation in the hearts of the Poles as is certain as those others. Dorothy Day and Peter Maurin, and Fr. Bruce Ritter, all of New York City, have anchored exemplary lives in the Eucharist, as have Jean Vanier of L'Arche and of course Mother Teresa. In arts and letters, the Faith in the modern age has nourished the glorious hearts of so many people: Hilaire Belloc, short story writer Flannery O'Connor, novelist Francois Mauriac, the prophetic and holy Leon Bloy, and Charles Peguy, the writer of those lovely tapestries; Dorothy Sayers was a Catholic, along with the poet of the Beats, Jack Kerouac, Edith Sitwell that distinguished author, and the dying Oscar Wilde; Dave Brubeck, Arlo Gutherie, and the repentant Giovanni Papini were Catholics, as was Aubrey Beardsley who created an entire graphic school; Evelyn Waugh the novelist was Catholic, and

his peer Graham Greene; and the celebrated playwright
Tennessee Williams at his maturity, G.K. Chesterton, and
sportswriter Red Smith; sculpter, tertiary, and writer Eric
Gill, David Jones the Welsh pencil and watercolor artist,
W.H. Auden and Thomas Merton; renowned author J.R.R.
Tolkein was a Catholic, and also writer Maurice Blondel,
Walker Percy an iconoclast, playwright Paul Claudel, Francis
Poulenc the composer, novelist Georges Bernanos, and also
Singrid Undset who won the nobel prize for literature;
Coventry Patmore was a Catholic, also Phyllis McGinley,
Spanish playwrights Jose Maria Penman and Joaquin Calvo-
Sotelo, the poet Francis Thompson, author and editor Dale
Vree, Alice Meynell, poet nonpareil Gerard Manley Hop-
kins, George Rouault who painted those famous canvases,
Edwin O'Connor, and the poet and friend of God Paul Ver-
laine; and remember Helen Hayes, and also if you can be-
lieve it, Salvador Dali the surrealist master. Catholics all.

At the frontiers of philosophy and the sciences, Catholicism presents the prodigal son Will Durant, Jacques Mari-
tain, Dr. Tom Dooley who loved the persecuted of southeast
Asia, phenomenologist and mystic Edith Stein, Gabriel Mar-
cel the existentialist, and Étienne Gilson; also the philosopher of personalism Emanuel Mounier, physician Alexis
Carrell, master-intellect Ludwig Wittgenstein, philosopher
Max Picard, and William F. Buckley, Jr.; and the economists
E. F. Schumacher, and Barbara Ward: Michael Novak the
publicist, historians Oscar Halecki, Carlton Hayes, and
Christopher Dawson; Romano Guardini, philosopher Joseph
Pieper, master-thinker Xavier Zubiri, Marshall McLuhan,
and the marvellous Malcom Muggeridge. And I'm tempted
to try to throw in Miguel de Unamuno. All, all are or were
Catholics.

Though some of these people came home late to the
Faith, each of them either now lives his life or has ended his
life as a practicing Catholic. Their example gives voice to the

wisdom and vitality of the Faith in our sad age.

But what of those apostates who've been among the most destructive of souls? Hitler, Gide, Sartre, Margaret Sanger, Simone de Beauvoir, Heidegger, Proust, and so many others were baptized in the Faith. It seems that lapsed Catholics are the most dangerous people in the world.

There's a reason for this, and it demonstrates that the Incarnation is plainly the chief fact of reality. The Incarnation—God become man—enlarges the soul. If Christ is banished after making His entrance at our baptism, there's damage done and a great void remains in the soul. Into that void, monstrous black tumours creep to linger and feed. They gnaw upon the soul itself, swelling abominably, filling the rightful home of life with deep-heaving thunderheads of mucuous and pitch. And a soul attacked like that cannot preserve itself.

The Incarnation cannot be eclipsed, nor can the Eucharist—the Incarnation remaining among us. Till the end of the world the Faith will sing *Dies Irae* over those depraved isms and ologies which proclaim its imminent death.

I once knew a young armor lieutenant of twenty-three who told me that within thirty years there would be no Pope and no Faith. They tell me has has died these seven years since.

Late in the afternoon, while it was still hot (the clouds had long since vanished) I came upon a huge limestone quarry where the massifs fell down close to the road. Across from the quarry was a restaurant in the midst of a good dozen concrete trout ponds. I entered around back, away from the quarry. In there I was alone except for the waitress and an anonymous clanger knocker in the kitchen. For an hour there was quiet and charcoaled trout and valpolicella, and also good white bread. Such opportunities in poor hurried lives are not to be squandered, as we both know. The meal and the quiet were each savory, in their own way. While I sat, the sky took the time to grow slowly darker, and then brighter and blue again. All the while I sat dreaming into the heart of the Dolomites in front of me, understanding something in the majesty of the world.

Without any provocation, the girl waiting the table walked to the juke box, pushed in 200 *lire* and punched three buttons. "Brick in the Wall" by Pink Floyd blared out. I might have sat still for Asleep at the Wheel that day, but not Pink Floyd. I paid my fare but I didn't leave her a tip. Had she been patient with me I would have. But as it was I carried my pack, my staff, and my dusty self outside.

The endless road ran straight down the center of the valley now. Meadows and row crops flourished to either side. Within a few hundred feet of the road stood red fir mountain slopes which hid in the snowcaps above.

To my left that afternoon as I walked I saw a young woman and her father sowing grain by hand in a little piece of plowed ground near a row of peach trees. She stopped to watch me pass, and she returned my nod with her own. Her bare arms wrapped a woven basket of seed. Though I couldn't see her perfectly, I fancied that she was modest and shy, and gentle. Four times, I believe, I looked around to see her watching me pass. There seemed a communion between us. A young woman's full dark hair hung to her shoulders. Her ample figure transformed those rude work clothes of denim and wool. How I wanted to quit the road and speak to her. But there's an art to approaching good women, and it's an entirely perilous business for a man. Remembering my purpose in Rome but regretting it with a pang as well, I pushed along, sadder, doing that young woman small honors in my heart. The last time I looked around, her father had set her to scattering seed again.

Since that day I've thought of her in a hundred hours. And I've hoped for her happiness. Perhaps, if she reads this, she'll know that I remember her.

The Italian road there bears the name given to it in that sad and quiet passage, which is the *Via della Porta Insuperabile del Silenzio*; to us who saw her and passed on, it is the Street of the Invincible Gate of Silence. It bent with the valley as both began to move southward now. In the narrow bends the wind gathered and took charge. Like a wind-harrowed serpent now the road descended, to become infested with thick, noisome traffic. At a hobble I made Primolano.

Primolano

I tried the first place that came to hand on the right, a place that I wasn't certain was an *albergo*. No sooner had I opened the door than I found myself facing a woman of forty or so, her arms folded, looking at me from where she stood at the end of a long dark room. At her side, a huge black german shepherd rose immediately and looked at me with menace. I called out to her timidly whether she might have rooms to let. The dog barked twice and growled, while the woman just looked at me. Remembering the swineherd who had once loosed the dogs on me, I backed through the door and closed it securely.

In a rough-hewn cubbyhole of an inn across from the church I rented a room from innkeepers who were rough-hewn as well. Even the red wine there, which is called *crinto*, was abrasive. After my third glass I asked the ornery, straggle-haired woman behind the bar what was the name of the wine again. *"Como se dice?"* I asked in very good Spanish.

"Vino!" she retorted, *"Vino vino vino vino!"* She spat the answer at me with her eyes and her fat hands. She thought I was a very great fool. But she took my money for another *crinto* anyway.

As it was evening, I finished my glass, went out to the square, and visited the church a little while. Our Lord was far better company than that in the hotel. Then I returned to the inn and read the Padua newspaper on the table, and watched a game of cards in the bar. Though I paid attention, I couldn't figure out the rules so I tired of watching and climbed the dark plank stairs to my room. Through the spread window panes, I watched the church tower and listened to the lovely talk outside in the dark while the warm air murmured with a resonance, so that it carried me away from the world for the night.

Ornery people are late risers. I was up before the woman. She only appeared after I was at the front door and ready to go, a little before eight. She was yawning and rubbing her house coat, shuffling about in her slippers, like a character from "The Honeymooners". She collected all of her money without giving me breakfast: it was too early for breakfast, you see, but not too early for commerce. I left with my stomach empty and moved onto a chilled, twisted road beneath the morning star. It was too windy to whistle so I had to keep quiet above the chin. The valley and its colors still declined, bent directly southward now. Scraps of blue skipped amid the clouds under sail. As I walked, the valley grew narrower and narrower so I buttoned my shirt to the top and jammed my free hand into my vest pocket. I pressed onward. By nine, the sky over the Valsugana had broken into pieces and all of Italy's blue light broke upon the valley.

From the highway that morning I saw Cismon sitting beyond its fields. On a salmon-colored house at the side of the village there seemed to be mounted a huge trophy: a green elephant's head. It demanded attention. Scrambling down from the leaves I followed a path into town to find not an elephant's head but a copper dragon—life size—mounted on the western wall of the house. And beside the house was what I can only describe as a surreal iron yard.

Cismon Ironyard

What a place! Mario's "Look and Find". "*IL CERCA-TROVA.*" The yard beside the house was wrapped with iron fencing, and filled with all that was incredible in metal:

shields and targets and graven disks, lanterns, reaper engines, old tractors, a throne, blades and plowshares, bed-
steads of iron and brass, grills, gates, pumps, old rifles, a sin-
gle-wing airplane, statuary, garden tools, busts of Mussolini
and Beethoven and I know not whom all, two complete suits
of armor, bird baths, picture frames, dinnerware, doors, and
a six foot high replica of Cinderella's glass coach. It was a
scene from the dreams of Salvador Dali, if Salvador Dali still
has dreams. I stood gaping. The Cleveland Wrecking Yard in
Trout Fishing in America came to mind. There they would sell
trout streams and waterfalls by the yard; here the crippled
Mario would sell them from his barber chair, but only if
hammered or cast of metal. The Cismon Iron Yard. *Metal
Working in Italy*. I think the literary possibilities are clear.

Mario could see that I was too poor and too immobile
to be much of a customer, so he ignored me. Fancy that. I
pulled myself away and came through Cismon by the main
street, past the white marble memorial which lists the dead
of two wars, then across a barricade and onto what used to
be the road south, now abandoned. An old, sour-looking
fellow in wollens overtook me with his scooter and gave me a
glance. He stopped at the roadside ahead. When I came up
to him he was picking buds from the bushes beside his
scooter.

"Bon diurno. What are you picking?" I asked just to try
my luck with him.

"Hops. Wild hops. These are used to make beer."

"You'll make beer then," I concluded dryly with a nod.

"No. I don't drink beer anymore. I use these to make a
very good soup. It's good for the digestion." He showed me a
handful of shoots he'd picked. "They're good when fried in
oil too. But today I'll make soup. I can't drink beer anymore.
My digestion is no good now." He touched his stomach with
a handful of the young buds.

So I left him there with a smile and a wave of my staff,

still picking leisurely at the bushes. He was a friendly man once spoken to, and it was rash to have judged him by his frown (as others are rash who judge me by mine). Perhaps his life was hard.

Just a mile or two beyond, in the church which stands on that little promontary in Valstogna, I saw an old woman whose life had certainly been hard. I'd stopped there at midafternoon to make a visit and to rest in the cool but musty nave. An old woman came in rather clumsily by the side door. She favored one deformed foot in a black boot. Seeing me there made her wary, perhaps because I was unkempt, and unexpected. But she hobbled noisily up the side aisle to a place where she could stand before the sanctuary. From there in the aisle she kept company with her Lover, and shared with Him that which was theirs to share. I was shamed by her patient suffering. My self-interested prayers were broken by her example: her whole attention was placed upon that altar. The old woman was practiced in the arts of intimacy and prayer. She took her time with Him. Only after she had attended to her purpose did she make a slow and more graceful walk along the aisle and out of the church. She glanced at me once as she left, and in her glance was no unease. Grace does that.

With her, imperfection was visible; with you and I it is more likely hidden. But God loves such people: the poor, the crippled, the passed-over, all those who suffer. One day her Lover will call her from out of the crowd and give her His arm, and bring her forward for all of us to love.

To think that such as she are interceding daily for the likes of you and me.

My throbbing left knee hounded me. But I pressed on and thought of that old woman. I twisted with the two lanes grown thick with traffic that often forced me into a ditch, leaving me not enough room to swing a dead cat. There was no shoulder here because the hills pressed in very close to one another like they were waiting for the doors to open. The noise of the traffic grew and I couldn't find the quiet needed for thought. My head was filled with the traffic noise. I worried quite a bit about my knee but continued downward anyway with the bending pavement.

Above me the day was bright with a brassy cast, but not sunlit. I kept my eye out for a place to eat but nothing was open: the bars had only the chocolates and liquor; the restaurants wouldn't open till seven; the grocers were all closed. I could only hunger and walk with that worrisome knee, and regret the untoward eating habits of the people of Trentino.

Slagna

At Solagna, so properly named, the sun broke upon that valley and cracked it open so that the hills were finally parted. As if at command the hills all fell down or drew back. I was free of the Dolomites. Behind me was the tumbled province of Trentino-Alto-Adige. Before me the sky stood tall and wide and far away over the colored plain of Veneto.

I don't mind telling you, I'm death on level ground! And here was level ground to make a walking man drool. I hammered for an hour toward Bassano di Grappa which I saw early on its solitary hill. The sunlit plain was more congenial than the dark slopes of Valsugana. I revelled in the hot light that warmed me through and loosed from me the shadowy grasp of mountain winds.

Directly I climbed onto the levee which reaches back toward the mountains from Bassano. It brought me in among the town's 30,000 people, beside a walled garden where church bells were ringing. I made quick to go in with several others. (Then as at other times I wished that I weren't conspicuous in my pack, my staff, my rumpled clothes.) With that Mass I did a good thing: I made my thanksgiving for passage through the Dolomites, and with them the Alps.

There's a wide belvedere at a corner of old stone walls in Bassano. Here you have a glorious view of the north. This hill of Bassano gives you a view of the plain and the levee road, beyond which you see the low and rounded forehills covered in timber, and the greater, scarred heights behind them, until in the farthest light you make out ices mingled with red stone just beneath the sky.

Couples promenaded arm in arm beside the balustrade. Several old gents sat quietly on the stone benches and took the early air of evening. I expect the array of hills would never cease pleasing those who have the good fortune to live here. It enchanted me, and I was for admiring it at my leisure. But my stomach demanded meat.

I came along the old paving stones, past the shops now

closing for the day. (A man afoot is at the mercy of others in the hours they work.) The only true restaurant I found was a dressed-up affair, and I wasn't able to tolerate the hassle I could expect there. Evening traffic was in full cry around the black-coated policeman where I passed him by the southern gate. I left it all behind me and came out the thoroughfare which made southeast across the plain for Venice. An hour later I found a hotel beside the road which had my one requirement: an earthy restaurant, and a clean bed.

Yourself: That's two requirements you had there, not one.

Myself: Not at all: I was counting in base twenty.

The waiter in his starched white jacket gave me a huge feed of beef, with barley soup, and bread, and fruit macedonia. There was chianti, and mineral water, and coffee too. I ate absolutely everything and ignored the bourgeoisie who infested the place with their frowns. The head man had parked me to one side of the door in my rough togs, the easier for me to be frowned upon. The bill was a fright but I paid and would have asked for more except that I didn't want to seem the glutton. I can eat a great deal at the end of a twenty-five mile day without a meal.

And I can sleep more than I can eat.

Cittadella is a fetching little town which would only exist in Europe. The wall of tan brick which embraces it dates from 1251, which is 25 years after the death of St. Francis, or 15 years before the birth of Dante. It admits entry only by gates at the four cardinal points. Each gate is a good 150 feet thick and fronts a bridge over the water ring, water stroked by white swans and black. The land all around is dead level so that the town lifts up from the plain suggestively.

The morning I was there the bells on the plaza were pealing. Though I didn't find Mass in the church (of course this disappointed me) I did find a novena to Our Lady. It was May after all, which is her month. The prayers were Italian but I could join in the *Regina Coeli*. I expect she approved of the white statue or her draped in blue velvet. She was paid that proper reverence which liars call idolatry. We the twenty or so faithful did our best to please her for a time.

Cittadella

Now, Our Lady has been driven to more and more apparitions in recent years to warn of the great chastisment that our vile age is inviting: Fatima in 1917, twice in Belgium in the 1930's, and perhaps at Garabandal, Spain in the

1960's. Most recently, there is strong evidence from the faithful that Mary appeared to children in August of 1981, at Medjugorje, Yugoslavia, to the great panic of the authorities. At this last site, they say there was a miracle of the sun similar to the one she worked at Fatima. There was the word *Mir* ("Peace") written across an evening sky in letters of light. A huge stone cross on a nearby mountain was seen spinning daily in rainbows of light. All these at Medjugorje, works by the Omnipotent Suppliant. At LaSalette we learned that one of her names is She Who Weeps. Wouldn't she weep now if she saw the shape the world is in. Doesn't she weep!

The sexton ejected me with the others, so I picked across the cobblestone square, now ablaze with the fire of the midday sun, toward a little cubbyhole shop to buy postcards. A demure young woman there with oaken hair was helpful. She marked me easily as a stranger, one meaning her no harm. I think she liked me. Once again I regretted my feeble Italian and fell back upon gestures and smiles.

In the town was an arbor with benches near the trees. I sat down on one and ate what little I had found to eat. Over the past two days, entirely against my will, I became an apprentice Hunger Artist. I just hadn't the good luck finding grocers along the road and I was loathe to scour the side streets of the villages afoot. I was hungry and the fierce daytime heat added to my discomfort.

Before me, as I sat on the bench nibbling, were the inner walls of Cittadella with the ring of water outside them. Over this water vaulted my road, hot and straight and flat, making southward onto the griddle that is Veneto. In the summer it's like this on the prairie, bright and hot and level. We answer to the light and to the wind just like these Venetians do. We live in a place like this broad Po Valley. We too are people of the South Wind.

For the next hundred miles there was, I think, not fifty feet of change in elevation, nor any lessening of the heat.

Out there on the flats beyond the town I came upon an old man watching me. He was before me, approaching me, and he dismounted from his bicycle. We met one another beneath a parade of huge poplars.

"*Bon diurno*," I ventured, for the old man had stopped.

"*Bon diurno. Tu pais?* Your country? *Tedesco?* German?"

"America."

"America? You have not walked from America, I think."

"No. From Bolzano. And before that from Germany," I explained. (And this was formally true, was it not?)

"Bolzano? You have come from Bolzano on foot?"

"*Si. A piedi.* All on foot. I am a pilgrim to Rome."

"Rome! On foot?" His old face lit. "You go to see the Holy Father, yes?"

"Yes, to see the Pope."

"*Bravo!*" he cheered, lifting an old fist above his shoulder.

"*Bravobravobravobravo! Bravo! Bravo!*"

Very full of myself and happy to be applauded by the old, who are wise, I marched off, stobbing for Rome and flourishing my staff, down the highway beneath those ancient poplars.

But my strength began to fail. I told you I hadn't eaten properly all day, and only eaten once the day before. What's more, the sky was threatening a late rain. But since Padua was only a short hour distant when the clouds arose, I pushed on along the road.

Just as I cleared the last town before Padua the rain fell on top of me. There was nothing to be done but to bang ahead. It proved to be a mistake. My strength and resistance had flown. I went slowly. The rain soaked into me. Lightning crashed and the water chilled me, crowding my body heat upward into my brain as a fever. With this fever then and worried for my health, I battled deeper into the storm and finally into the dark *impasto* of night. As I struggled I remembered my ruin in Bronzolo; and I feared. The storm allowed very little progress. Two long hours later I staggered into Padua in a tearing black rain, weak from fever and cold.

Before Padua

Two inns at the edge of town turned me away to wander in the rain. Nearby a bar was filled with Italians my own age who catcalled after me as I dragged past in the rain. I was ailing badly and in a foul mood, so when they called after me I wheeled and walked in to make trouble. "I wonder what else they can do with their mouths," I thought. Of course they all quieted when I entered, and paid solemn attention to their drinks. I looked a very rugged piece of work. All they could see of me was a bearded scowl, my thick staff in my fist, a dripping poncho, and rude boots. (I've seen professional wrestlers who looked similar as they climbed into the ring.) Standing close enough to drip water onto the likeliest heckler—and he now quite mute—I jammed my staff down near his feet, clenched both my hands atop the staff, then leaned toward him. With as menacing a face as I could manage, I asked in German, "Have you a room free?" (I guessed he wasn't the innkeeper, nor was he German. But it was my way of challenging him.)

As I expected, he shifted backward from my poncho, and shrugged toward the barman. Between them all, they gave me to understand that there was a *pension* just up the street, across from the train depot. And more than that they wouldn't say; they only sipped quietly from their glasses.

Returning my attention to the chief heckler, I pressed him for confirmation (I told you I was in that nasty mood.) "Is that true?" Is there a *pension* across from the depot?"

"*Si. Si,*" he offered, but no more.

"How do I know whether they have a room?"

He managed a nervous smile mixed with embarassment. He said nothing, and just shrugged.

"*Bene,*" I growled. "*Grazi.*" I turned widely around so as to splatter others with water, and walked into the crashing black rain. This time there were no catcalls, but only murmurs behind me.

Across from the depot I found a hotel which was the House of the Cossacks and the Holy Ghost. There the woman gave me a bed in a fifth floor dormitory that was little more than a garrett under the slant roof. I slumped into one of seven empty beds, and endured a Night of Infinite Resignation, which precedes the Night of Faith.

There in that garrett I prayed and tumbled the night through. The horrid memories of my sins troubled me. For these I dealt with God late into that night. As I wrestled with the fact of my wasted life I asked, "whatever will become of me, and my poor tattered soul?" My answer was the mystical gift of tears.

The fever broke early in the morning and I slept until ten. Then I went down to my breakfast and out into the streets to see what I could learn about this lovely Venetian town where Petruchio met and wooed his Kate.

Architecturally, the 13th Century Church of the Hermits (the *Eremitani*) is more interesting to me than the Basilica of St. Anthony. It's tremendously old, built forthrightly of brick in the Lombard style. The roof is lifted by dozens of parallel black wooden trusses which define a ceiling of seven stacked barrel vaults above the long nave. Andrea Mantegna adorned the Church with perhaps his greatest works, the frescoes which were painted around 1455. His worm's-eye view of *St. James Led to His Execution* was masterful, to judge from the remaining pictures.

But the Basilica of the Saint is the goal of pilgrims to Padua. Its six domes remind me of the byzantines and St. Mark's in Venice. It holds the tomb of St. Anthony, who died young, and also a marvelous portrait of St. Maximilian Kolbe, who took the place of a husband and father listed by the Nazis for execution. St. Maximilian's portrait is imposing: the priest is shown transfigured, a man's man confronting the darkness of our time, beneath the open arms of Our Lord.

There in the basilica I saw an old man go dragging past, a man who seemed to me the exemplar of mankind. He was old and bent, though once tall like mankind, no longer robust nor handsome just like mankind, dressed in an old overcoat and carrying a cap in his hand. He was in church, where we do well to be, and he was at ease. Shuffling up the right hand aisle he found himself before the chapel where some of us were hearing Mass. He paused and genuflected with attention and then continued on about his business. He did honor to the tabernacle and then occupied himself with other fish to fry. He and God were on speaking terms, and he was at home in this splendid Faith of ours. The old man was at ease in the basilica. He belonged there, as we all do.

Out from Padua I marched, and crossed somewhere that line along which the city was besieged by Bayard, the last true knight of Christendom, "knight without fear and without reproach." All day I pounded across Venezia in pulsating heat and glare-light, mile upon mile over the flat land without a horizon. It was a hot, blistering, shadeless bone of a road. That sky beyond Padua is sharp when there's heat; it cuts all the way to the ground.

Yourself: I don't know about you but I find this Venetian heat oppressive. It's hard to walk like this for such a long way. My feet are sore and I'm sweating and I'm tired.

Myself: There are worse folks you might travel with, and greater difficulties you might meet than these.

Yourself: Name six.

Myself: I'll name only one, and that an example of such power as will put an end to your whining.

Not many years ago, in the Spring I think it was, the Devil undertook yet another tour of the world, this one an American lecture tour to promote a new collection of his writings. And a horrible, hard time of it he had before he was through.

Yourself: Was he walking?

Myself: Hush and listen.

Yourself: I thought not.

Myself: Anyway, all the major universities of course vied for his time, but he chose to begin at Notre Dame, having been elected Senior Class Fellow there that year. As befitted his importance, a full week of campus activities marked his visit. He was lodged in a tower room in old Sorin College, the tower farthest from Sacred Heart and closest to the bookstore. He held afternoon humanities seminars with the dean's list students and the student government mandarins. There were feature articles all week long in the student newspaper, and photographs taken for the yearbook (which didn't develop). He autographed copies of his new book each morning at a table on the quadrangle in front of the bookstore. Excerpts from his works in theology, economics, and politics appeared in a souvenir edition of the highbrow magazine. As a mark of general affection for the Devil, the student academic commissioner personally introduced him at each function, using his pet name, "Nick." The Devil was a hit.

That Saturday evening the library auditorium filled early with those who came to hear him give his major address: "The World and the Flesh—*Apologia.*"

He was stunning. His poise and delivery were flawless. He was a haberdasher's dream: banker pinstripe, Italian shoes, pocket kerchief, a razor-cut van dyke, and a tasteful pair of dress horns. The Devil spoke at length, enchanting and delighting the crowd. By way of summation he told a clever little story at the expense of Our Lady's virtue which was warmly received, and then closed to the hearty applause of the assembly.

As is customary after major addresses, the house lights went up and several hands were raised. The Devil recognized one well-fed, tweedy man who wore an Egyptian pendant around his neck, one of those theologians that are kept around Notre Dame for effect.

"I feel certain," he began, "that all here agree that religious truth" (here the Devil winced) "and religious certainty" (and winced again) "are intolerable, each being the diseased fixation of a narrow psyche. Will you please share with us your estimation of how the evolutionary process may be accelerated to bring us beyond truth and certainty to full relevance? Thank you."

"It's a long dialectical process," the Devil began, "too intricate for the time we have to discuss it here. Perhaps you would care to speak with me later." He walked to the side of the stage and leaned forward. "Here's my card. Please contact my secretary for an appointment." The theologian took the gold and silver card into his two hands reverently and returned to his seat, where others ogled the card and passed it around.

Another hand went up, but before it was recognized, beneath it rose "Brother Jimmy Ray Haskins, servant of the Lord and pastor of the West Side Universal Brotherhood Church of Get Out 'My Way in the Name of Jesus. Whoop! My, but I feel good tonight. I'd like to ask all the brethren here to hold hands and join me as prayer shock troops, in reading witness in Scripture against Satan."

Well you can imagine the indignant protests of foul play from the crowd, but onward Jimmy Ray launched at the top of his voice. He began with scattered clauses from the major prophets. Next he read phrases from here and there in the letters of St. Paul, and after that snippets from Revelations and Acts. All the while the Devil stood quietly behind the podium patiently whisking his tail, smiling back at the embarrassed faces in the crowd.

It took a while but Jimmy Ray exhausted his familiar sources of Scripture and was faced with quoting directly from the four Gospels themselves—something contrary to his normal practice—when, as he drew breath, the Devil interrupted.

"Vinegar Bible, I think," he said.

"Huh?"

"I said that's the Vinegar Bible you use, I believe. Is there a parable of the vinegar found in your bible?"

"Of course," returned Jimmy Ray.

"Of course," smiled the Devil.

Arms yanked the puzzled preacher down to the floor. His protests were muffled by the applause. Hands went up again.

Before he could choose, the Devil found his elbow in the firm grasp of an erect man at his side. Dressed in black slacks and a white shirt, the man's green eyes gleemed beneath his gray hair.

"Hey, Bub!" (which is the diminutive form of Beelzebub), "You're the Devil are you not?" he said, staring directly into the ruddy, blinking face.

"I am," came the puzzled reply. "And who might you be?" he asked, eyeing the crowd in amusement.

"Simon Thibault, a Dominican tertiary."

The intruder spat squarely into the Devil's face, grasped the demon's elbow tighter and, raising his own right hand, began "I baptize you, in the Name of the Father; and of the Son; and of . ."

Kablam! Up blazed a roar and a commotion, a storm of screaming wind. The walls shuddered and the floor buckled. The lights went out. The room flashed hot. Pop went the

Devil in a blast of sulphurous red heat, knocking the audience out of their seats.

When the smoke cleared and heads poked up, only a pile of cinders remained beside the intruder on the stage. The Devil was gone.

Thus ended abruptly and untidily the ordeal of the Devil on tour. So, Yourself, if you think that travelling with me is difficult, consider how hard it would be for you to travel with the Devil when there are hardball tertiaries about. Count Yourself lucky.

Yourself: That tertiary was a poor sport.

Myself: The Committee for Academic Freedom thought so too. They barred him as *persona non grata*.

Padua

There were only quiet little villages that afternoon below Padua, all of them nondescript and plain faced, rather
dusty, parched, and strung along the road south. There were
stretches of wide land, much of it in summer Durham wheat
which these Italians will grind for pasta. I passed into and
out of these heat-silenced Venetian villages at will, meeting
resistance not from the road but from the hot air which anes-
thetized Italy. Between the towns now there were irrigation
canals which gave off the dog days stench of stagnant water.
The sky swelled and burned overhead; it rolled a horrible
hot light down onto the asphalt. By three o'clock the Italians
were inside at their *siesta*. The shops were closed; the blazing
roads were empty; no one stirred in the villages. I walked unseen through several of these, carrying away southward
nothing but the dust on my boots, and silent images of these
bright but hidden southern places.

By four thirty, people were abroad again and the sunlight was cooling in its early decline. My road shuffled past
the gate of a shaded manor at the edge of one of the villages.
Behind the gate was a young paraplegic with a yelping rat
terrier at this feet. He was taking the air under a huge elm.
He gave me a big wave and a grin, and I returned with my
own. We showed our fists, for strength, yet his strength was
the greater. For him and for others I had a duty to walk well:
on behalf of all those who cannot.

My road lurched right then left through Bagnoli along
toward evening. Two teenage girls, one of them in yellow
slacks and blouse, breezed past me toward town on a Vespa,
honking and waving. At either end of town great and ancient

Italian maples lined the road. Along the eastern shoulder, these had been brutally topped out, leaving tall trunks without limbs.

Beneath these in the soft air, I came upon two lovely, regal women, about thirty years each, on their evening *passeggiata*. Languidly they strolled in their tailored blouses and their long summer skirts, rolling their hips ever so gently, with their arms linked as European women will. One of the women bore raven hair to her shoulders; the other's was titian. Both were lovely and very proud, for which it was hard to fault them—and since it was hard, I didn't do so. They wore their beauty well, and they were not to be hurried. Neither woman would acknowledge me as I approached, which was fitting perhaps. They passed by, returning toward Bagnoli, leaving me only to ache and to wonder after them.

Lord save me but they were beauties. And in such an out of the way place. One never knows.

Anguillara

A fine Italian evening was abroad when I made Anguillara, Anguillara which was made to order by God. I entered the village's only restaurant and, finding myself alone but for the wife, her child, and the young owner, I stuffed myself full of fried pork, some red wine, and a few pickled eggs from the bar. But when I came outside again to mix with the five hundred people there, I found they had all been driven indoors. It had begun to rain. So, reversing my first choice to sleep rough I hunted a room.

Directly I found my way to the little tavern and hotel, where there now was no room. The owner said he could do nothing for me. He shook his head at the rain outside. "*Bruto,*" he said.

It was growing late and the rain was steady. Believing that a priest can't turn away a pilgrim, I crossed the square to the rectory beside the church and made my pitch to the priest while standing in the downpour before his doorway.

"Hello Father . . . no Italian . . . pilgrim . . . Rome . . . all on foot . . . German . . . twenty-five days . . . See my map . . . Trent, Padua . . . Yes, my tent . . . but the rain . . . hotel full . . . late . . . (pitiful look)." You get the idea.

He turned me away, sending me disappointed back across to the hotel. There the answer was the same as before so in five minutes I returned to finesse Padre Roberto. This time we made friends. Properly suspicious of vagabonds, he became convinced at last of my authenticity as a pilgrim and so he allowed me to sleep on the upper floor of his school. But first he took me into the church where we gave short prayers of greeting and thanksgiving to God. Then he led me to another tavern, beneath the parish school, where I was introduced to the barmaid who would show me where to sleep. She sold me wine twice and left me to myself at the bar for thirty minutes. Then she gave me the keys to the school when I asked for them.

After I was bedded down, about ten perhaps, Padre Roberto appeared in the school and spoke to me. "Would you like to come with me to the rectory? We could have some coffee or some wine and you could tell me about your adventures in your walk. I would like this if it would please you, and if you're not too tired."

"Thank you, Father," I said wearily. "For me it would be better to talk in the morning. Today I've suffered a lot from the heat and hunger, and then from this rain. But I'd be very happy to talk to you in the morning. What time is Mass tomorrow?"

Early the next morning, Sunday, he woke me with the church bells and gave me breakfast. He announced me to the women in the pews from the pulpit at Mass. I wowed 'em there in Anguillara. So many women and even two men wished me well on my pilgrimage outside after Mass. To some I gave promises of prayer in Rome—promises I kept. The priest and his housekeeper, a kind old woman with very bad teeth, gave me a *viaticum* of chocolate-covered biscuits, biscuits I wolfed down before Rovigo. His final kindness to me was to send two little boys out to guide me a few miles past a tricky road junction: two quiet children, "like little hills of silence," Max Picard would say.

I knew then that I'd been lucky when it had begun to rain and I came into the company of the good curate of Anguillara.

It was Sunday in Venezia. Father said the people had a dialect—which would explain the altercation that Belloc got into in Venezia eighty years earlier. I had the road to myself. The women were back from the early Masses now and at their business in their homes. The men I expect were still asleep; the fools don't attend Mass usually in Italy. Anyway there was no traffic to speak of in the district, over which moved only myself and a morning breeze, very cool and bright.

I made three villages southward while the road turned, Tinkers to Evers to Chance, with nothing much on my mind but a morning walk abroad in this lovely Italy. In the third of these I came upon a queer family: at least I think they were a family. They were Four Sorrowful Mysteries. Two dark women at once wild and fearful were walking the roadside, with a similar little girl between them clinging to their colored skirts like the little child Hope that Peguy wrote of. Before these three strode a tall, angular, dark man in a soiled overcoat and fedora, with children's yellow sunglasses perched incongruously on his nose. As he walked he kept his hands clasped behind him, except that he waved silently to those few he saw working in their gardens beside the road. If they ignored his greeting he pinched the bulb of a bicycle horn that was tied at his waist, and waved again. None of the four gypsies spoke a word, but they walked in sorrowful silence. They were all poor and very crude. I remembered the Travelling People of Ireland, and one I knew in particular, a boy named Paddy, now grown to manhood.

Pray for God's protection of outcasts, so little befriended by the world.

Toward Presella

The blacktop, shining beneath the high angle of the afternoon sun, skirted east of Rovigo and glided further on amid the flat fields and the bloated canals and the tree lines. Great shiny cottonwoods stood beside the road and shaded it from what was by midday a sweat-pulling heat. And with the heat in this low-land near the sea came the regular discomforts: glare of course, stifling humidity, sunburn on my neck and arms, blisters, the drone of insects (in the fields, I mean, not in my head), and the smell of sweat which wasn't much different than that odor rising from the stagnant water in the canals. I slunk from shade to shade regretting these hours in the sun and these miles in the light. The road was like a knife edge. There was nothing for it but to pound for Rome. Pounding (and pushing and stobbing and banging) for Rome was the only way.

How hard it is to coast when you're a foot pilgrim. There's no automatic pilot, no rolling momentum, no cushioned ride, not even any right-of-way to judge from the way the drivers act. Every mile must be covered by force, by sweat and grit. And when that grit is spent, the walking man will not make one inch more, unless he collapses and rolls down an embankment into a river and is washed out to sea. But in this case he doesn't get where he wants to go—which is to Rome, isn't it—by coasting. And there's the physical lesson from the physical experience.

This same physical reality which disables walkers also tosses a stick into the spokes of those like the wry, cycological Phaedrus in *Zen and the Art of Motorcycle Maintenance* to bring him to earth in the physical world. "Quality", indeed. What a bunch of hooey.

The endless road stretched atop a sun-gashed embankment which stood up to climb a levee beyond a basketful of parched, white homes. Below the road was a formal, rectangular garden of hedges and fruit trees on a lawn. There I found a green slat bench in the shade of a barren pear tree. I

lay on the bench and studied three green lizards at play in
the heat. (Lizards don't work do they?) For a good half hour
I slept; then the heat woke me and for a while I just lay
there. At length the fierce sun pushed the shade off of my
bench. I found I was causing a certifiable stir among the
mothers there. Pairs of them passed by on the gravel path to
investigate the vagabond on the bench. Seeing the stir, I
shouldered my pack and moved on. I think it was kind of me,
considering the fierce three o'clock heat, and given that I
was famished.

Polesella lay ahead of me, fronted by a field of new-cut
alfalfa. I dragged myself on burning feet toward it and toward the dam of the river Po beyond. In a dark little bar
there, the first one I saw on the shady side of the street, I
took the conversation of a Sunday afternoon with a tableful
of men playing cards.

Polesella

Yourself: Oh, you talk to everyone. Admit it now: you do.

Myself: Well, God talks to everyone. I don't see why I shouldn't do as much.

I gave them a reprise of my march while I swallowed one warm beer and then a second. While I told them of the world, there entered a man of sixty, quite tall and well groomed, his hair combed back, wearing glasses. He caused a great commotion among the others. Greeting them and then me, he sat down at my table. The others, who deferred to him, told him what had been learned of me. Then he spoke to me.

He was the sage of Polesella, this man, *il penseroso*, and he was a real character. He seemed their intellectual dean. I found he possessed the habit of generosity, because when I finished my beer he offered to "buy if you fly"—a bargain anywhere. What's more he told the barmaid to give me a glass to drink it from. I tell you he had class.

"*Salute*," he toasted. I answered with my glass. We wandered in *lingua franca* over whatever pleased him. He was plainly driving our talk and I was only riding along. Scorning religion because I was a declared pilgrim, he did prove thoughtful upon the remaining universal themes: "The whole world is my home . . . I'm a brother of all mankind . . . It all comes out in the wash . . . Don't wear two fragrances at once . . . Every wine is the typical wine for my region . . . All political parties are corrupt . . . Government leads to war . . . Nothing can be done about the weather . . . Commmunists are swine and Capitalists devour the poor . . . Don't water the wine . . . I am a leg man." And, "Can you lend me a thousand *lire*?" You can see that he was a thinker.

With the sage, everything had an amusing ending. His conversation was a fancy of Italian and French; and laughter. But the laughter was of a melancholy turn which I think was owing to his intimacy with life.

It was as though he was saddened when I got up to go. Telling him briefly of my intention to make Copparo by night, I shook his hand and we said good-bye. But I didn't know then that he was also an adept moving pick.

At the end of the street is Polesella's hotel plaza and fronting the plaza is a levee. Climbing at the left as the sage told me, I rose onto the bridge which vaults the river Po. Dozens of Italians were strolling on the bridge's sidewalks under a lavender sky in the customary Sunday evening *passeggiata*. Many young couples walked arm in arm. Teenagers pushed infants in strollers. Dignified young women strode languidly in pairs. Children bicycled erratically in twos and threes. Tiny Fiats crawled forward with young men leaning from the open windows. The Italians were taking their ease with one another and with the river. Later, by night, they would all go home to their dinners.

The Po River

Some of the rivers of Europe might better qualify as creeks on the prairie. But not the Po, which separates Venezia from Emilia-Romagna. It's a river supreme, an ancient of days. It's blue water, not brown, and it needs these

open spaces. The Po is massive compared to the great
Danube where I'd crossed it in Germany. Moving with the
dignity that befits its station, it washes eastward into the
Adriatic some forty miles away. Here at Polesella it's a titan
hundreds of feet wide and unruffled by any commotion, the
master and chief of its district. Grassy bulwarks stand up fifty
feet on either side of the water, but if the Po should turn its
hand against its neighbors, I see nothing that could withstand
it.

Twice more later that evening I saw the Polesella sage.
The next time was in this new province of Emilia-Romagna,
with its flats and irrigation canals. For all my carefulness I
had mistaken a wide indirect route for the road to Copparo
and found myself haplessly tacking left and right over the
road network, with Copparo visible in the distance. The land
was so flat that there weren't three landmarks to reckon by:
only the spire and buildings of Copparo beyond.

Two bicyclists in racing togs found me wandering there
and corrected my route, pointing out the short way around.
By way of conversation I told them where I had been. I
slapped my good hip and knocked my good foot with the
staff. They were amiable guys, rounders, and after a good
time. Both were truck drivers for a dairy company. They had
lots of girl friends they said. Right there on the road they invited me to go dancing with them that night at a place where
a good many pretty young ladies would be found.

Yourself: Please, let's remember ourselves.

Myself: Certainly. In fact I know a little versicle which a
man told me once by way of guidance with women like these
guys were looking for:

> We don't smoke and we don't chew,
> And we don't go with girls that do.

I'd just told them that I would go dancing (because I

wasn't tired at the time), and had set off, when the Polesella
sage rode by on a Vespa, waving at me and cheering, inciting
me on to greater effort with one pumping arm.

Two long hours later I dragged my bones into Copparo
much sorrier to look upon than that clear, pastel evening arriving above me. Perhaps five thousand people live in Copparo. It's large enough to have three major streets and a
square where sit buildings a good four stories tall. A fat boy
with a frisbee led me to one of these, and there I found the
pension recommended by the bicyclists, the *pension* at which
they would call later to bring me out dancing. It was after
nine and the kitchen was almost closed, but the innkeeper
gave me spaghetti in the dining room and a litre of cola. It
was my first meal that day, and it was coming very late. But I
didn't eat it in peace. The cyclists appeared. I had a knotty
time of it begging off for my weariness. They'd cleaned up
and put on their best clothes and they wanted to show me a
good time. One of them even had a sport coat. But beg off I
did and they left reluctantly after some minutes.

As they went out through the bar next door, I saw for
the third time the Polesella sage. He came to my table and
greeted me in English, which he hadn't spoken earlier.

"I came this twelve kilometers from Polesella just to see
if you would arrive in Coppara tonight."

"I don't look as good as I did earlier, but I made it," I
mumbled through the spaghetti. I offered him some cola
which he declined.

"I see that you have, and that you're now in the hands
of my good friend here, Gino, the innkeeper." This same
Gino appeared and reminded the sage that the restaurant
was closed. The sage nodded and turned again to me.
"Please, forgive my disturbing your meal, but I wanted to see
for myself that you really are walking all the way, like you
say. You are, I see, and I congratulate you. It is very unusual,
what you are doing. *Arrivederci*."

"Good night," I answered. "God bless."

That was the last time I saw him. As we shook hands he smiled that melancholy smile of his. We'd gotten on well. The old man was a practitioner of that fidelity which is called friendship, and he'd have been good to know.

In the morning, I padded around town in and out of shops for awhile, not buying much of anything and not meeting anyone. On certain mornings I'd found it very difficult to face the road. This was one of those mornings. It was at least ten o'clock and very bright when I wandered to the edge of town. Before me lay the curving gray road, the wheat fields to either side, an anonymous house or farmstead here and there, and a very tall sky heavy with heat which pressed the horizon flat in all directions.

The brutal heat of that high summer sky was absolutely crippling by the time I hammered into Tresigallo at eleven. My tendons had swollen shut (if tendons do such things); at least they were very swollen. That morning to try to fight the heat, I'd only laced up my boots half way so that they flapped against my calves. Within the first five miles my heels were swollen. I needed a rest when I made town.

All of Tresigallo should be levelled. That would be the best thing to do with it: level it. There's precious little human comfort there, an excess of cranks, and a want of trees as though they were desert Arabs. What few trees there are on the main street have been disfigured by a topiary maniac. Maybe it's all so queer there because the town is an oven. Everything in Tresigallo is stone and asphalt and brick and orneriness. When the sun is high, the town and everything in it is cooked through. That day the sun was tall and ferocious.

I wanted to visit for a while in the church but it was closed and the pastor wouldn't open it for me. Even the priest in Tresigallo is short-tempered. So I grumbled and walked to the shops where I sat under the blue canvas awning of a bar to eat and better yet to rest. A bald, fat man who was sitting outside and sucking a popsicle spoke (or rather shouted) to me, I couldn't figure out what about. Maybe he was the *major duomo*. Or maybe he was the bouncer. He just kept shouting and waving those popsicle sticks. Once I'd finished eating I closed my eyes and feigned sleep. Soon the fat man relented.

Tresignllo

That day I'd seen signs pointing to the Adriatic twenty miles eastward, and to Ravenna, the jewel, perhaps forty miles to the southeast. My mind took to consideration of Ravenna and its Byzantine glories from the age of Justinian. In Ravenna you can see those celestial mosaics which prove that the Byzantines understood that light was a stone which could be quarried: it could be shaved, or chipped, then fixed in place. Those stone ceilings in Ravenna prove that the Byzantines were journeymen in the medium of light. But now their art has nearly been lost: there are so few masters remaining.

Tell me, why is it that we've lost the glorious art of illumination, the art which, like so many others, rose to perfection at the court of Constantinople, and in the monasteries of the Middle Ages? Why do we have books without illumination? books with mere graphs and tables? books with photographs? Why has the worthy profession of the Illuminator of Manuscripts passed from among us? It's a cause for sorrow. I wish it weren't so. Perhaps it will return when all other good things do, in the End.

It must have been that infernal heat of Tresigallo that roused me after a half hour under the awning. I gave a curt *"Ciao"* to the fat man (who waved another popsicle) and a second *"Ciao"* to the company under the awning, and then I dragged myself wearily back onto the baking pavement, across the glaring flats for Rome.

My spirits improved after three-quarters of an hour of heat when I found a Lombard chapel in a wooded garden beside the way, across the highway from a decrepit manor house. It was made of Roman brick from the 12th Century, which brick is so much longer and shorter than ours. The good people there had lately restored it to glory. The scents of mortar and wood were abundant in the small room. One slender window set in each wall let in a fragment of dusty afternoon light; otherwise, it was like a cellar in there. Votive candles flickered on a bronze stand. I stood in the cool and stale air, leaning upon the head of my staff while I gave petitions and thanksgiving before the tabernacle. While I stood there praying, the curate who had been alarmed by my appearance looked in to ensure I wasn't a vandal. He was right to do that. I understood his concern so I moved on. The briefest visit in the tiny sanctuary was all I needed to put me right. I knew it would be.

You wouldn't expect this but the way across the Venetian basin is quite a vexation. The basin is laced with canals brimful with that wretched stagnant water and those frogs and the leaden air. The roads pick their way, catch as catch can. I did maybe five miles along the latticework to gain no more than three by line of sight. What's more, my heels were horribly swollen. All afternoon I hobbled and sweated and grumbled beyond Tresigallo, and cursed the false engineers who had laid the roads of Emilia-Romagno. I also cursed the locals whose neglect to plant trees along the roads caused me discomfort. All I could do was limp ahead and sip on a warm bottle of grape juice I'd bought somewhere. Lucky thing, there was no one handy for me to harangue.

Somewhere beside one of the canals, two boys in soiled hand-me-downs and muddy galoshes joined me from the lane of a decrepit farmhouse. And two stranger boys I haven't seen. The older one, about fourteen, looked like a morose Jerry Lewis. His younger brother, just as morose, was the plump one of the two. They both just looked at me as we walked. Neither asked any questions. They didn't speak to me or to each other. They just walked and looked. The light was missing from their eyes. I tried to make conversation, but neither of them said a word. I suppose they walked beside me for at least a mile. Then they began to slow, but only a little: they slowed to one pace behind me, then to three paces, to five paces, then to ten paces behind. As I turned now and then to look at them, they dropped further and further back. Before the second mile, I couldn't hear their galoshes any more. But onward they came, watching me. At one place where the road tacked leftward I looked back and they had vanished. Absolutely. I think they had made for one or two hay barns in the fields.

Now what do you make of that?

Yourself: Say, they were different. They remind me of that family of strange people on the road below Anguillara. Do you suppose they were related?

Myself: Maybe. The look in the eyes was the same. But I really don't know what to make of them. Not at all.

Late in the day I found a man. He was tall, perhaps forty, muscular and tanned, tow-headed, and he was stripped to the waist. He was raking hay with one of those long wooden rakes of dowels and pegs. It was he who spoke first.

Yourself: Ah, a mesomorph. A classic specimen if I ever saw one.

Myself: He was nothing of the sort: he was a son of God.

"*Bon diurno,*" he said with a move of one brown forearm. "What's your country?" I answered him and he asked again, "Where are you walking?" I stopped and fished my map out of the front of my sweaty shirt. I showed him the line of march upon it from Schesslitz. If my map had been long enough I might have claimed a beginning at the North Sea, I was feeling that ornery. Anyhow at my evidence he whistled and slapped his leg soundly.

"All on foot? Where do you sleep and eat?" he asked in a rough German.

"Yes all on foot; *solo a piede.* Oh, outside when it's fair, in *pensione* when it's foul; grocers and restaurants and *tavola caldas* and *trattorias.*"

"How I would like to do such a thing," he said with a wistful far-away stare over the top of that rake. "But I have a family as you see." He motioned toward his smiling wife and daughter who were sitting on the porch of the house beyond. Seeing them there, beside him while he worked, it was I who envied him.

"*Fiele man!*", he offered, looking me in the eye. "Much man."

Grinning, I lifted my staff and one fist to confirm my spirit, and pounded off toward the south, sweating and carrying the heat of the afternoon.

The day wore on. The miles of flat meadows and water ditches came and went. At evening I came under a placid sky, but one flat and very dry, and then into the sea district town Portomaggiore. Its streets are wider than necessary for the number of people there. The town is misnamed: it's not large and there is no door.

I suppose they have very few visitors there except for those in the hospital because I was gawked at more than usual. One old fellow looking on told me of a place where he suspected I might get a room at a *"precio buono"*; and there I could tend to my swollen heels. This first fellow passed me on to a second old man walking by with his bicycle who detoured with me to the *pension* and rang the doorbell for me (which was unnecessary of him). That was all I saw of Portomaggiore that evening, except for the geometric garden in the town square that my room overlooked.

The rest of the town I saw the next morning. The pavement led out from town, wandering like the little breeze lifted from the sea beyond view, and then wove along slender water ditches beneath the trees. These last were a waste that early. The harsh sun of the day before was missing. There were mallards in the water ditches who quacked at me as I lumbered past. Blessedly there was no traffic. A workman was patching the road with asphalt from a truck bed. Beginning with an exchange of the morning's pleasantries, we leap-frogged forward repeatedly, as he drove then stopped at a pothole then drove forward then stopped. It was a nice diversion for me.

Yourself: Some people are easily amused.

Myself: It's a gift.

At a turning of that splendid morning road I found myself in Consandolo, something notable with its big fruit market on the church lot. I chatted there with an orange and plum vendor (I mean a vendor of oranges and plums, not a two-colored vendor; anyway . . .). Then I bought orange juice and some yogurt for breakfast from the grocer at the corner. I'd awakened the innkeeper that morning to pay him, and no breakfast was to be had at the *pension* before I set out.

Though it was just early morning, not yet nine, my tendons began to creak painfully as in the day before. And the clear morning threatened more heat, which would certainly find its way to my feet.

Yourself: You and your tendons: beef to the heels like a Mullingar heifer.

Myself: Enough of you now.

By the time I made Argenta I was damned near lame. Slumping onto a bench in that long park there I started to consider riding to Forli, only to Forli, about a day's walk ahead at the far side of Emilia-Romagna by my reckoning. I could barely walk. My heels wouldn't flex at all. Across the square was a church toward which I hobbled, thinking to pray. But it was closed and so I went into a bookstore instead where I bought a pocket dictionary in Italian. The woman recommended it to me if I should need a tool for talking with doctors or druggists. Finding the word for "pain" in the dictionary eased my mind some.

Back on the bench I fretted. "I've only had this pain since loosening my boots for ventilation. Maybe the remedy is to lace them completely again." I laced both boots all the way to the top. At the end of the laces I tied knots and at the end of the knots I tied bows, just like Tinkerbell. I thought, "I might yet be able to avoid riding to Rome if only these tight laces do the trick." At that I stood and shifted onward painfully, creaking stiff-legged and stiff-footed, until the numbness of the road set in again and I could swing without pain. Familiarly enough there was no real horizon ahead of me. There was only the asphalt, and the grass, a few elm stands, and of course the heat.

We do well to remember from time to time the banality of Good and Evil. Both are mixed intimately with every human pursuit. There's no deed whatever which we may not sanctify to our help or defile to our harm. Earlier on this road I'd fancied in vanity that it would be nobler to ride to Forli at the foot of the hills and walk from there up into the Appenines. "Who'd be the wiser?" I asked. It was pure nonsense. God values each day's march, each day's fight whether glorious or not. To please Him we offer this hour and this effort, we live this present common moment. God, say His friends, little values grand intentions of sanctity for a later day. It's only these present hidden moments, these present dry miles, forgotten beyond Argenta which He asks of us. He asks this little span of hours between now and Pentecost.

Only fools equate sanctity with enthusiasm, and religion with theatre. It's in our procession of little moments as much as in our bursts of celestial passion that we're to hope for mercy.

I'd walked 550 miles since Schesslitz, and perhaps 200 miles since Bronzolo. I'd come as far as the *Via della Macina della Tristezza*, or the Street of the Millstone of Melancholy.

Just beyond Biagio (which has more trees than most of these towns, though it's just as flat and pekid), the road swerved to the right of a plantation of poplars, past a collection of workers picketing a mill, and up onto a grassy levee that overlooks the river Reno. On this side of the bridge I found a large elm with a small lawn beneath it. I was weary and gant, though no longer in pain. The afternoon was drowsy. I lay down and slept there in that shade beside the Reno.

Drifting in and out of consciousness, I saw the afternoon sky lose some of its ferocity and take on a dappling in grays and whites. Across the road, an old man sat tilted in his chair against the green shutters on a tavern. He was eyeing me. I picked myself up and tramped ahead, past a cemetery and toward a gathering of houses: not farms and not a village. In front of one of these houses a slightly built man of some forty years spoke up to me in English. I hadn't seen him until he spoke.

"It's a hot day for your walking?" he asked. It was his English that surprised me.

"Hot enough anyhow. But I've learned to get used to it. I've been at this for some time now."

"Come on, sit down in the shade by my house and I'll bring you some very good wine. I have red wine in the cellar behind the house: a lambrusco. It will only take a minute to get it. You wait here and I'll bring it to you, and then we can talk. Come sit down."

Since we'll all be a long time dead, and since I am susceptible to kindness, and since the conversation would be in English, I didn't hesitate. I took to the bench at the front of his house.

My host poured for me freely and I drank as freely a rich lambrusco which he boasted was made there in that house. His wife and father-in-law joined us with a second bottle at the ready. There the four of us sat talking of places we'd been and of others not to be missed. They had lately watched "How the West Was Won" on television and they all wanted to travel to the western United States. The woman and her husband were teachers; the old man was a retired truck driver. The wife took my map and made a mark upon it in her own hand. Next to this she wrote "Giovecca", the name of the place.

Their hospitality was easy. We drank their red wine and kept company with one another, the four of us, out of the sun's heat. But when I was refreshed I made ready to go. The wife gave me a *vade mecum* for the walk: a full bottle of that lambrusco of theirs (which had to be opened carefully they warned, and was tied with twine), and also a bottle of white for variety. Happier and heavier by a litre of wine, I left them there in Giovecca, whom I would never have met had I ridden like a coward from Argenta. It was a good thing that I hadn't been a coward.

Yourself: The wine, was it good?

Myself: Well the lambrusco leaked all over the inside of my pack, and left a red stain on half my belongings. What little was left was good and true enough. As for the white, well it was white.

Yourself: Ah, yes. Wine is such a profound thing; especially the white. Truly.

Myself: Yes, truly.

Long before I found the wine leaking I was given a choice at a fork in the road: Lugo to the left, or Santa Agneta dead ahead. I chose Lugo and for that I'm to be applauded, because it was the more demanding distance. The pavement lifted and crossed the Santero river which flowed northeast, forsaking its spring in the high hills of Emilia-Romagna. Along the river there were olive groves well tended. The land grew more animated in the distance now, where there were hills at last, and trees upon the hills. I caught from a distance the subtle variants of the countryside, owing to that delicacy bred in me by life on the prairie: A life on the subtlest of land forms and the most instructive. There's a refinement of temper required in order to appreciate the prairie. You must learn to guage her temperament from the merest suggestions, from glances and nuances, from her velleities. And if you befriend her you're the richer.

Though my road still lay on the flat of the Po plain, the baked Venetian marl was mostly behind me. Tomorrow promised a look at the Appenines.

At a second fork in the road a blue sign pointed left for Lugo, but I played a hunch that the shorter way was straight ahead beyond the detour. I went straight. I was wrong.

Moving no quicker than the oncoming evening, I hobbled along a series of gravel roads, each moving at right angles to Lugo as though to a tornado. Beyond the freight yards and the vacant lots, I came to a workman's hotel in what was the Matt Talbot part of town. They gave me a room on the third floor for three dollars. I tell you, that room was as large as the dining room downstairs. It was a dormitory. Below in the restaurant I had a meal fit for a stevedore: beefsteak fried in olive oil, and everything else from wine to coffee. Since it was Italy there were bread sticks instead of rolls. There was a cruet of vinegar on the table. I rubbed the vinegar on my sunburns when no one was looking.

That night I learned my lesson about why some rooms are cheaper than others. The rowdies in the bar downstairs caroused the night away until three in the morning. At that hour, a hard rain broke upon the Emilian night, and everyone made for their homes.

The rain lasted until daylight, nagging yet impotent, neither bleeding nor healing. Beneath it I came through the low hills and trees, land which I say lately appeared in greater relief. I was tired that morning after only five hours of sleep, and I would rather have slept all day. The earth was growing wakeful again, Emilia-Romagna stirring from the sleep of

Venezia, adorning herself in folds of green and straw-blue haze, raising up on one elbow some little ways into the air, an olive and wheat *odalisque*. Above her floated a guaze veil which hid her somewhat from me, and me from her. Feeling more than seeing the wakeful land, I came along in a weariness to Faenza.

Faenza Centro

It's a big town, Faenza. Factories and warehouses lurk about the perimeter of the town. I wasn't intimidated and in time I made my way among the bent streets to where I found the *centro*, the cobblestone square which sits beside the bricks of that old church there. Colonades of a hundred yards bound the square on either side, and behind the colonades are deep porches. Behind the porches are the shops. The air was dingy in Faenza. The pavement was wet with the occasional mist. A broad canopy of yellow canvasses floated over an open-air platform where the girl in the ice cream shop served me sandwiches and beer. I sat there with my feet on one of the chairs and studied my new Italian dictionary. When the drizzle stopped and I was drier, I pushed up that road which carries Faenzans to Forli.

Yourself: I'll bet you a nickel the weather doesn't hold. We ought to stay here and eat ice cream. It looks like rain to me.

Myself: You're right. Not ten minutes out from the town I hit a hard rain. Beating a tattoo up the side on the glistening asphalt, I fought spray and blast from the roaring cars. The march to Forli was a total horror: wet and cold and traffic-ridden. But as every lawful penance has its term, this one also ended—at the city gate.

Workmen had lately plowed up the streets at the western gate of Forli, leaving a muddy soup underfoot, and causing the cars to snarl and splash about noisily in the evening rush. Pulling up short at the muck, I waited for the traffic and grumbled. An old gentlemen stopped beside me, heeling two slender hounds with a tug on their leashes.

The old man volunteered a comment to me in Italian.

"No it's not! It's mud," I fired back, in no mood for any nonsense.

"You are English?" he asked, startled.

"American."

"I was in America: 1956," he began.

We compared notes while the traffic cleared. There was no waiting for the mud to clear. He took me to a place where we crossed easily into the town, into that city where the flag stone streets narrow and turn at all angles. Past their four stories we walked, while he collected food and wine for his supper. Somewhere on one of the streets he found me a hotel, and then invited me to eat with him at his home.

I agreed. His apartment was in bachelor disarray, so I was comfortable. There the old man cooked dinner for which I thanked him; he said to me, "You do me the real courtesy by joining me for supper."

We ate a plain meal, out of the pots as bachelors will. He'd basted a chicken, and with this he'd boiled nested noodles with butter and cheese. There was a flat bread, a specialty of Forli, stuffed with spinach and cooked in a waffled iron; and blood red oranges of the kind they call

"sanguinara". All of this we took with a good red wine, San-
giovese (of Romagna)—more noble even than Beaujo-
lais—which he'd bought in honor of our dinner. When I
drink the red wine of dejection I remember him. And his sorrow.

Late into the night that old man and I sat at his table as
at a loom, and wove of the strands of our yearnings a conversation, gracious and dark, a mantilla to cloak the hearts of
two men. I could speak only my flax, but the old man spoke
silk.

His wife had died suddenly only three months earlier.
"She took sick in the plaza of St. Mark's in Venice and died
within two weeks," he said. The old man had loved her and
he was disconsolate. But he was a Catholic and so he still
had a family and a home. We discussed the news of the
world somewhat that evening, but his talk continually returned to his wife. Many times he declared to me what a
prize she had been, and how few there were left like her
nowadays; and that he had loved her.

In a little album he kept photographs of his wife. He
had it close at hand, on top of the bureau. Mixed with her
pictures were poems they had written to one another
throughout their marriage. He translated one of these for
me, one he had written to her, pausing at times to find the
right word in English, or to wipe his eyes, or to clear his
voice. Some of the words I missed. But I saw plainly that he
had tried to be good to her, and that he would not have
missed life with her.

He was desolate now. But he was good and he will go to
Heaven. He will be with her again. God grant to every one of
us what had been granted to him: long life, and health; and
happiness. And love.

In the morning I changed the last of my money into *lire*
and fell in love at a druggist's shop on the plaza before
strolling out from the town. I intended to make a light day of

it and march only as far as Meldola, not an inch away on the map, there to sleep rough or fine as the weather allowed.

Forlí Centro

Here beyond Forli another light rain fell. Further off, a mist thickened the air. Still I could make out the silhouettes of true hills appearing just beyond the town. Quietly, I passed out of these last Emilian lowlands and came up to mix with those hills which are answerable to the Appenines.

For my road I chose a small wet pavement which wound some and rose some through the mist, moving southerly as it was inclined. Emerald grass not yet headed with grain carpeted the fields, beside that taller living hay which stood upright in others. The lift and resistance of the road challenged me. I plodded ahead in my own sweet time and gathered my expectations upon the mountains.

For a diversion from the monotony of the mist I sang myself that song, so widely praised, wherein we can at once amuse ourselves and take instructions in math, manners, perseverance, and even inventory management (something important, what with the price of money nowadays).

Yourself: What would that be?

Myself: I'm referring to what scientists have proven to be the most human tune in the world. I begin it now in the key of C.

99 Bottles of beer on the wall
99 Bottles of beer
You take one down and pass it around
98 Bottles of beer on the wall.
98 Bottles of beer on the wall,

Yourself: Stop!

Myself: 98 Bottles of beer.

Yourself: Enough!

Myself: You take one down and pass it around . . .

Yourself: !

Myself: I ran out of bottles of beer before I ran out of road, so I scuffed quietly toward Meldola (and why its accent should be on the first syllable I don't know). It's an inoffensive enough town beneath the hills, with a rock quarry below it on the outskirts. The road which had been gently going took a crimp and a crease, rising sharply from the quarry. I took it up into the town proper, up beside the colonades which attended the street beside the shop windows.

Yourself: Folks hereabouts are mad for colonades, aren't they?

Myself: Apparently so. All those shops were closed, which was great for my wallet: all but one hotel bar sitting at the upper edge of town, where the wet countryside reappeared. I went in.

Five local men were passing away the damp afternoon in talk and drink at a few red formica tables. I bought a beer and drank their health, and then I talked about my adventures as was my custom. For amusement I lied about how cheap my boots had been to buy, boots they all seemed to like. But the conversation was slow and so I asked for a room.

"*Pieno,*" a man said with a wry grin.

"What?"

"*Pieno.*"

I flipped through my dictionary to the P's where I found "*Pieno* - full." Damn.

"Is there another hotel in Meldola?" I asked.

"No."

"Close-by then?"

"No. Not close."

"And the next hotel?" (Now it was beginning to rain.)

"Galeata."

Galeata was twenty miles by the looks of my map. Although I knew I could do the distance, it was a blow. I didn't want that march just then. I'd planned to rest early there in Meldola but I was now to drag myself once again into the rain, and along that darkening road upward to vanish into the evening. It was closer to five than four o'clock by now.

There was very little shoulder to the road, and the heavy traffic aggravated me. Muddy trucks carrying gravel from the quarry struggled up the hill past me. Emptied, they rolled downward to the quarry again. I slogged up the mud shoulders for some six or eight miles. A young mother alarmed at my approach brought her little girl in from play on the porch and peeked with her from behind the curtains. I smiled. She was a good mother to guard her child.

A tiny settlement appeared with no shops and only a nasty knot of hillocks for the road to twist through. It lifted upward again, rising higher onto the hills beyond. Dark trees ranked themselves on the slopes and gathered into small timbers. I was thirty minutes getting through one large wood before the rain stopped. There was brush and hedge about and the dim fields in grass. One beyond the other they gathered upward, while the neighboring Bidente churned down-

Cosercoli

ward in disarray

At Cosercoli the river widened, then feinted to one side before making a rush under that long bridge there and over the dam. The town clusters in the elbow of the river and looks onto it. Evening Mass bells rang as I sloshed in. As always I was in need of spiritual care. But it was dark and nearly night, and it looked like rain again; the road ahead was ominously unknown. Parishioners filed into the church for Mass while I stood and debated. A fellow nearby in front of the church volunteered to me that there was an inn but three miles further. I decided. I pressed on.

For that last hour, the rain deepened the darkness. Any true light left the sky. Both heaven and earth grew sombre and dim so that the two became one. Only the rain had voice, and it just whispered while I moved up the road.

At eight o'clock I found the inn where it was to be, among those last rising hillsides near the Marches. I took shelter there and found light. And I found good, human company with a woman who displayed a picture of Paul VI. For a fair price, she fried pork for me in olive oil, and two eggs. Her daughter, who was plain and shy, brought me soup with some bread and a glass of beer. All the while the rain fell upon Romagna, calling us all to sleep.

That day, which was to have been a holiday, had been a common ferial day with a twenty-five mile forced march in the bargain. It just goes to show that you can never tell.

Christianity is a subset of Catholicism. This pedestrian truth contradicts what we're taught in the prevalent anti-Catholic traditions. In America, we're taught to regard Catholicism as one amid a multitude of competing Christian formulations, and a rather backward one at that. The truth is the opposite. The truth is that Catholicism is the meaning of Christianity. A religion will be Christian only if it retains some portion of the Catholic deposit of Faith.

Only our apostolic Church keeps sight of the truths of God and men: the Incarnation, the Resurrection, the Eucharist, the Passion and Death, the Mass, the coupling of Scripture with Tradition, the Communion of Saints, the Sacraments, the efficacy of Prayer, the complementarity of Nature and Grace, the wedding of Faith and Works.

No, to be fully Christian one must be apostolic, be Roman. The others substitute a part for the whole. Take away every Catholic thing from these others and what you have left is paganism. Outside of Catholicism it's useless to speak of a common Faith.

Imagine that the Pope were to announce one Tuesday morning that he had been down in Gide's Caves of the Vatican and had learned that all the claims of the Prussians' Higher Criticism were correct: that he'd found all the notes and drafts which had been used to create the New Testament, which was a late creation of the 4th Century A.D.; that there had been no Christ as we know Him, no crucifixion, no virgin birth, no resurrection, nor ascension, no anything. Also he knew how the Shroud of Turin had been forged. Imagine that he were to say that Christianity had been a colossal hoax, and that every good thing which had been taught the world by the Faith was no longer defensible. Suppose he said that he was going out to get drunk, and that everyone on earth could do exactly as he pleased without objection from the Pope. Why, the lesser churches of this world would be out of business by Tuesday noon. And by Tuesday night the permanent darkening of mankind would have begun. No good thing could live in the firestorm which would follow. We who would be left without our anchor would turn in every direction and savage one and all; we would "have them down" in their board rooms, their offices, their clubs, their city rooms, and their shops. Everyone everywhere would be fair game.

Without the Church, kindness and truth and sanctity would desert us forever.

Catholicism means Christianity.

One little village I came across in those Emilian summer hills that next morning had been erected of stucco and gray stone. It was crowded onto an outcrop of rock in the Bidente. From its perch it peeked over the edge at the river rushing by its feet. The buildings were all gathered tightly, permitting no spaces between their walls. The church bell tower was foremost near the river. Nothing passing on the water could avoid view from the villagers' windows. The walls looked down like a crowd of ogling gray pigeons.

There was soft rain that morning. Green hills and their kind rose abruptly in the narrow valley. Because of the constricted view, I could see no true mountains yet. But trusting, I carried upward toward the Appenines of which I had read and heard men speak.

Yourself: What had men told you of them?

Myself: Please. As Dr. Johnson said, questioning is not the mode of conversation between gentlemen, and you seem to be forever asking questions.

Galeata appeared and faded like a guest who's late for dinner, yet eager to be early for the theatre. In it were more of the familiar arcades fronting shops, none of which were notable. Indeed there was little to remark about that morning but the fitful rains and the gloom, which clouded the figures of those hills. The land was a pale panorama of wet vineyards, of upturned wheat fields, with timberlines so far away. Without much effort I passed higher to a ridge line from which I looked down onto a little town which sits in a cellar at the foot of the Appenines, Sophia.

The men I met there laughed at me when, as I sipped their tar-like cappuccino, I told them I knew for certain that I could walk across their Appenines. Ridiculing me good naturedly, but ridiculing me all the same for even wanting to try, they pointed out the street which would bring me onto the upward road to where the valley splits there beyond Sofia: one arm eastward for Stia with the Bidente, the other to Rome. Doing exactly as I was told, I found the road of their warnings. From the town I saw it climb steeply and tortuously, bent to its purposes.

Just as I began the climb, a little past noon, an old man with his dog riding beside him pulled up short in his dump truck and offered me a ride. Before he stopped rolling, I sent him off with a left-right wave of my staff. He had a hairy time of it getting up steam again on that incline. He must have known well—but I had no idea—how much mountain there was to come. And how many passages: one at Carnaio, the other at Verghereto.

The high lands leading to the first of the passes have pushed so many ridges up through Romagna, like bones upon which old flesh has settled. The earth here is of several kinds: fertile green pastures and grain fields on the gentler slopes; rough brush with trees on the steeps; and pale earthen scars on the many sheer faces. The houses and sheds have become orderless in their placement. They've scattered over the hillsides. Squat stone homes and sheds sit wherever the land seems most nearly level.

The Appenines

Upward I zigzagged, into mists which glided like condors. Massive vapors sank into the valleys and farmsteads below me so that the green depths were hidden. I dragged myself higher for a mile; and then for two miles; and then upward for two more miles; and even for two miles higher yet. I stopped neither to rest nor eat in all those hours. Whether there was mountain rain or mists, always I rose, the stillness more and more intense.

At Monteguido ("Mountain guide," appropriately) I exchanged greetings with an old man collecting pigeon eggs from his coops just below the road. There was a very small hamlet built around one lone inn, where the road passed from the leeward to the windward side of a rising arm, so that the gorge passed to the right from my left.

It's sometimes good for us not to know the size of the efforts we undertake, else we might not undertake them. This is surely true when a climb is seven miles high. Time and again I reasoned that the vapory line before me was the pass at Carnaio, only to gain the ridge and find yet another line higher and more distant. At that I could only collect myself once more and tramp upward into the stillness. The crest was like an asymptote I approached without reaching, hour upon hour upon dreary, tromping hour. It was such a long brutish pull upward into the silent heart of that mountain.

At a bending in the road, I looked across a two hundred foot gorge toward a building or two seeming to be against the sky, so high were they with only Heaven beyond. I dropped disgustedly (what a trial it is to go down when we want to go up) and climbed up the far side of the gorge, then dragged myself into the bar I found there.

"To the four of us," I toasted them with a slender glass of red wine. "What's the name of this place?"

"The pass: the Passo del Carnaio. The top is only another hundred meters further up the road," answered the bartender.

Near Passo del Carnaio

From Meldola the afternoon before, I'd climbed 2,500 feet. One ridge down. Only one more ridge remained to be crossed twenty miles further on before I bested the Appenines at Verghereto.

Like the barman told me, the road rose another few feet to a ridge and hesitated before it descended to the last towns snuggled in Romagna. From the pass I saw far below me San Pietro in a vapor and the road which led around by the valley to where I thought Bagno di Romagna would be.

My spirits brightened there on the pass after the four hour climb. I gloried in my victory. I wanted to share my triumph with others in the town below. Not waiting for the road to lower gradually, I tore ahead and downward, lurching and sliding across a wet meadow, then plowing a lower field of young oats, and slogging through the tiniest stream of brown water. In minutes I was down to the town.

Two old fellows I spoke to on a street there laughed when I was faced by a huge wolfhound on the loose. They

S. Pietro in Bagno

shoved the dog away, and then quarreled over how far it was to Bagno. But I didn't care. I'd long since learned that folks would always claim that the distance I expected to the next town was wrong. It proved to be a mere hour's pace through a damp evening along the river Savio. The water was swift now because of the earlier rains that day. The cool air was damp. Just as I made Bagno the church bells announced evening Mass. When they stopped, I questioned two women walking behind me, then ran to the old parish church on my swollen feet, and happily got Mass for the first time in days.

Bagno di Romagna

Across from the church was a fine hotel (also named Savio) owned by a young couple. The woman was my age and so was her husband. She served me a handsome meal which was given all her guests that night. She said I had no choice except for the vegetable. But that was all right. I'm good-natured. I battened on it.

While I ate she took my map, which I was studying, to mark places on it that I should see on my way to Rome. She gave me special attention because she saw I was wounded from the walking. After the supper we few guests sat with the wife and the little girls while the innkeeper built a fire in the hearth. Some of them played a game which I took to be Rummy, while I watched and drank their wine. In order to discharge the duty we have to entertain as well as be entertained, I told them about far places and wonders and long, marvelous marches under the sun. There was the old flavor of repose in that room, and just enough silence to do us all good. We passed a quiet, companionable evening there: beneath a crucifix and before a fire, in that valley known as Romagna, between the two ridges of the Appenines. And sleep that night was good.

The gracious wife was anxious to see me filled up at breakfast, knowing that I was bound for Rome afoot. She gave me as much of the rolls and coffee as I pleased, more than she allowed all her other guests put together. She kindly wished me well and reminded me to see La Verna, the mountain where St. Francis received the stigmata. (You see she understood something of the things which sustain pilgrims.) But outside Bagno my map sent me elsewhere. I turned southward and up toward Rome instead of westward for La Verna: toward Rome as always: toward Rome.

There is a lovely, rising valley above Bagno which carries you through the remnants of Romagna and on to the ridge. Sometimes a cold wind moves along the bends in that valley, as does the odd cloud. When both of them are abroad they chill a man so that he buttons his collar and pulls his cap down lower; he shoves his hands into his pockets and squints into the mist. Since the land is steep, it burns his legs with the strain of the climb. There are no settlements, except one, in all that long lonely climb of better than three hours. A great unfinished expressway perches on hundred foot stork legs and struts from side to side. There's very little traffic, for people haven't much reason to go there. Only an uncommon purpose will bring a man upward alone through that secluded and meditative valley, where Wisdom journies among men.

The glow behind the mist moved higher. Toward midday the land rose less steeply. Against the palor of the sky clung the ragged town of Verghereto, perhaps five thousand feet above any sea, marking the southernmost summit and reach of Romagna. Beneath the town was a shameful tunnel put there to cheat us of completion in our efforts, as if the long climb didn't count. After rising two thousand feet that morning the road skulked under the hide of the pass, no more than fifty feet below the sky.

Anticlimax being one of the trials of life and one of the chief marks of the human condition, I accepted it all. I crossed through the Appenine ridge by the tunnel, to gaze onto Tuscany and the downward roll into Rome.

It was another and a wilder country spread out below. The cold air whirled over a savaged wasteland: deep washes, and pastel gullies, eroded gray rocks and soil. What life there was clung to the lumpy rises between the washes. Wiry little pines were knotted with the scrub brush. It's from this rugged cradle that the young Tiber rises. And there I found it: going down, nobly, even at its young age, between the soil washes on its way to the sea. At its high fountain it appears in bright green which turns white near the rocks. The water moves with dexterity between the hillsides. Some few of the hills further down are in grass, but most of them have suffered from erosion.

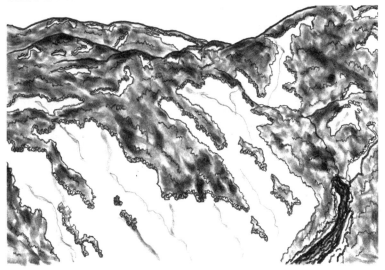

The Tiber

Downward I jolted with the pavement amid the jumble of hills and hill rocks, past the brush or the trees. As I walked I wondered how long it might take for the water beside me to reach Rome.

Beside a westward bend sat a coarse, once-grand house of rocks and a decayed garden beneath the trees. A decrepit grape arbor overhung the doorway. Inside, the house was what the outside suggested. The balding innkeeper himself presided in a costume of both worn clothes and new. Fleshy tumors grew beneath his eyes, which gave him the pestilential presence of an outrider of the apocalypse. Before I'd sat long at my coffee and bread he prospected me as a lodger for the night.

"Are you walking somewhere today? Where will you stay the night?"

"Yes I'm walking to Rome. I'll stay wherever I can when the hour is late: in a hotel most likely, tonight."

"This is a hotel here. We take lodgers," he offered.

I remarked the early hour yet, because it was only midafternoon. He yielded and grew quiet.

A farmer strolled in and ordered wine, then lodged his hands deep in his pockets. When he learned from the innkeeper I was a celebrity, he bought the two of us wine, which pleased me a good deal. Another farmer entered in knee boots splattered with old mud. He also learned of me from the other two and bought the four of us still more wine.

I'd been quiet while the others talked. As I finished what little bread I was eating the room grew quiet. All four glasses were empty and the eyes silently shifted my way. It was my turn to buy.

Well, I beamed handsomely at each of them in turn, and rose with a flourish. They smiled. To all of them I addressed English quite pleasant but direct. I went promptly and conveniently stupid. "I expect you can't understand me now, and perhaps that's just as well. I want to thank you both for your generosity to me. The wine our host has provided us was delicious. It was a courtesy for which I believe you will all one day be rewarded. However I'm a poor travelling pilgrim, you can see, and I have only the money in my pockets. When it runs out I'll be broke. I can't be buying drinks for all of Tuscany."

I picked up my pack and staff and, with a genial wave, walked out from the house and onto my road. It may be that I heard one of them grumble. I left them poorer by the cost of wine but richer for the memory of our meeting. For my own part I carried the episode with me toward Rome and the Fisherman.

Both the afternoon and I descended. The sun appeared and warmed me, as had its younger brother the wine. I merely had to shudder to move downward, it seemed: so pronounced was the slope. With this minimum of effort I came to a settlement called Pieve, midway through a day's walk down from the crest. I'd made no towns whatever in those four hours from Bagno di Romagna until Pieve in Tuscany.

Pieve sits in a modest plain where the great hills part for a wide holding of fields and meadows, where people can gather and live. It's the first town beyond that roughage of upper Tuscany where I found the Ultramontanes, so famous for living beyond all mountains. They're a more passive and settled people, these Ultramontanes. Their towns are neither large nor notable, neither rich nor poor, and they carry on admirably without the likes of you and me.

There is one church in Pieve and one other lesser thing, a sanctuary. The church is maybe two hundred years old, of a rough cut limestone. Its floor stones are worn from the tread of all those worshipers. In there, in the quiet, I prayed, while evening entered the church from the street.

Not far south of the church was a tiny stucco hotel, not two windows wide at the front, packed between the stone facades of two taller businesses. They all shared a flagstone square with a bank, and with a druggist's, and a half dozen small retailers. The old woman at the hotel had a yelping terrier which she left below in the parlor by the television while she showed me to my room. Her lodgings cost nearly nothing. She had no other boarders, that night, nor did she seem prepared for them. She was poor and it was clear that there were no meals to be had there. But she'd furnished the room generously with such poor furniture and prints as she owned. (Sadly, the old woman has closed her tiny hotel since.)

From my balcony I watched men playing *bocce* ball well into the twilight in a dirt court beside the river. I watched them long enough to guess the rules and to know which of them were better. They went quietly away by ones and twos with the last light. I lay down and listened to the dark Tiber washing southward.

In the morning I was away early. Hardly anyone was awake except the old lady and me: the whole town was asleep. I came out from Pieve on a little road which cut into the shoulder of a dozen fertile hills. There was no more rock to be seen in them. The land was in vineyard or trees. Some of these latter were the curious umbrella trees, looking like their namesakes blown up inside. The first face I saw that morning was that of an old Tuscan hunkered down atop his wooden cart, coaxing a grey draft horse north toward the mountains. I think he was as surprised at me at that hour as I was at him. We greeted one another cordially, with waves and a smile. His was the easy gesture of a farmer who's accustomed to courtesy. We carried past one another, each on his own way. I thought about him and how a more natural, Distributist, draft horse society than our own can't be all bad.

My plan was to make Sansepolcro, some ten miles away, for Mass at ten. This left me plenty of time to have an admiring walk of it through the low green hills, paired as they were with the azure sky. So I strolled at my ease up that beguiling road, through the shining air. The southern sun warmed Tuscany. An air came very broad and rich, as though from woodwinds held by the gods, woodwinds announcing the theme of a Tuscan aubade.

Faint Mass bells surprised me after a handful of morning miles but I knew it couldn't yet be Sansepolcro. I hustled up a lane beneath some umbrella trees and then under the little brick bell tower just off the road that was nearly hidden by a shed. There I found a chapel filled with Tuscans at Mass. As with other chapels in Italy, the altar pedestal covered a third of the room. The altar itself was an outsized boroque affair of cornices and pillars with scallops. And as in other Italian churches, they sang *bel canto* a moving hymn to Our Lady—*"Vesta Con Noi"* I think the title was—with a curious syncopated refrain. After the Mass we all followed our

Before Sansepolcro

priest outside where a little shrine to Mary stood atop a pillar near the shed. The priest prayed on our behalf, which is proper, and blessed the fields in all four directions with holy water. Then we all went away, having done what is ageless and good for us: having pronounced benediction. They went off through the morning to their homes and I walked on further into Tuscany.

Past the chapel my road rounded a hillock, beyond which a vast plain lay spread, with Sansepolcro upon it and a gunmetal sky above. Sunbeam and shadow coursed broadly about the plain. The light was all the more striking because I saw it from the shadows which covered my hill. The land glowed. It seemed lit from beneath. The plain was filled with waving tree lines, vast fields, with buildings scattered and gathered, and the town itself, all randomly placed. Pale hillsides were barely visible for their haze, even though the day was pretty clear. There's an old Jimmy Webb song, "The

Yard Went on Forever;" the plain of Sansepolcro was like
that yard. I stepped down onto the plain and toward the old
town's northern gate.

Sansepolcro is settled into the accumulations of its long
prosperity. Stout dressed stones rise fifty feet over the
streets, where that morning the well-tailored Tuscans were
taking the air. Pacing between the shaded cobblestones and
shops, I heard the tattoo of martial drums, which drew me
with a crowd to its source. We found there the town's cathedral on its tilted thirteenth century street. Down the street
marched a procession of medieval drummers and banner
carriers, all in the old colors of Europe. The young men carried heraldic banners from their right shoulders, and cross-
bows and horns, preceded elegantly by young ladies in lavish
empire gowns. The company drummed down from the
cathedral street, and across the square nearby, then on toward the ancient brickwork on the south wall of town. I
know because I saw them there as I was leaving later. They
were gathered on top of the tower in a ceremony of some
sort. None of them paid me any mind. Anyway I went into a
shop to get postcards. There I knocked some people about
by accident with my pack and was sent out. So I sat me down
a while to eat on a park bench beneath a statue of Piero
della Francesca.

A native of this part of Tuscany, Piero della Francesca
was a great painter of the early Renaissance, a specialist in
those frescoes which were so popular then. His figures are
grave, blonde in tone, and even heroic; and in some sense
you could say they are translucent like his era. They possess
an emotional gravity which makes their gestures those of a
race arrived from the sun. They say that Francesca believed
in scientific perspective as the basis of painting, so much so
that they say he's perhaps the earliest ancestor of modern
abstract artists. That's what they say.

Yourself: Well, what do you know. He was quite some

painter.

Myself: And his statue was some statue. But back to the road.

Rains appeared as I made the highway, to fall for upwards of an hour. Water loitered on the roadway, soaking into my boots in the bargain and making me walk near the crown of the road when traffic permitted. It was a matter of pressing over the flatland to the rhythm of my staff. Since it was cloudy and raining, I can't say what the countryside thereabouts looked like: visibility was only a quarter-mile or so. My poncho did me little good. The rain was everywhere. It found the seams in my poncho and blew in with every little gust from the wind. It was only the level going which kept my spirits in reasonable repair through the middle hours of the day. Such was my introduction to the legendary charms of Umbria.

They say that St. Teresa of Avila was mired down, oxcart and all, in a thunderstorm. She was bound on some business on behalf of God and was fed up with the problems He was sending her. "If this is the way you treat your friends, no wonder you haven't many," she chided Him. She could do this because she was on good terms with Him. I never heard what Our Lord responded.

Anyway, using my standing as a pilgrim, I sent up petitions for a rush end to the rain, with the reserve clause that I intended to walk on to Rome even if it rained the entire way. I was now a week out from the City by all reckoning.

When I'd covered the three miles to Citta di Castello it had stopped raining. And therein lies your lesson against fatalism.

The streets in Citta—at least the ones I walked—were torn up for laying sewer pipe. On one of them, I was flattered when a pretty blonde recognized me from earlier on the road. She'd been waiting outside a roadside bar for someone or other. That loden dress of hers was a perfect complement to her figure. She almost smiled at me as we passed. Almost but not quite.

Hopping about among the holes and the Umbrian mud I saw what the artists call umber laying in a narrow arc of street between closed shops of every sort. The street led to the cathedral, which also was closed. So, I found another very human thing: a corner tavern nearby where I got bad wine and tiny sandwiches and a look at the Monte Carlo auto race over the shoulders of the crowd. The barman was dressed in one of those starched white linen coats. He smiled warmly and shortchanged me skillfully. This put me in a cross mood as I made southward for Umbertide. Above me hung a clearing midafternoon sky, while I tromped into what my map confirmed were now the graceful, the supernal hills of Umbria.

Before Umbertide

Yourself: Umber. Umbria. Umbertide. Umbrella trees. I'm bored! What's more, this southern sun is a furnace.

Myself: What do you think would entertain you.?

Yourself: I don't know. Maybe if we talk some. I need an intellectual challenge.

Myself: Why don't you suggest a topic?

Yourself: To tell the truth I've been thinking about something these past few miles. How many people do you suppose we've seen on this walk?

Myself: People we've seen lately or people on the entire march?

Yourself: The whole way. How many people?

Myself: Oh, counting the crowds at the beerfests, the people driving on the road, those at Mass, and all the people in the guesthouses at supper time—maybe a million. I don't know exactly.

Yourself: Me either. But there have been a lot of them. Still, the world doesn't really look overpopulated. I know that the "experts" say that overpopulation is a problem, but I have my doubts.

Myself: Careful, now.

Yourself: Think about it. There are 5 billion people in the world, give or take a few. From my old architecture studies I remember that there were standard space requirements for various types of facilities: so many square feet per person, and so on. And it turns out that if you seat all of mankind in one place for a party, and everyone has as much space as in a fancy restaurant lounge, you can seat the world's population in less than 3,000 square miles—and every one of us with plenty of room. You can even throw in kitchens and bars and planters full of vines.

Myself: That's not much room.

Yourself: It's less than 60 miles per side: only ten days' walk around it. Corsica is considerably larger, and Israel much larger than the space required. Perhaps it will be like that at the Judgment, when we're all together at last.

Myself: So the problem isn't really that there are too many people, but too little sharing of what there is.

Yourself: Hasn't it always been so.

Myself: Always. And here's a wrinkle for you along the same lines. The age of mankind would seem to be much less than the million years commonly cited.

Yourself: Now that's inflammatory. Everyone knows mankind is millions of years old.

Myself:: Not if you look at the numbers.

Yourself: What numbers?

Myself: Five billion as current population, and an average rate of population increase somewhere under two percent yearly. Those numbers.

Yourself: I don't follow you.

Myself: It all has to do with compounding, like in finance. If you take a beginning human population of two people a long time ago, a present population of 5 billion, and an average rate of one-tenth of one percent yearly, then it only takes 21,000 years for the first two people to increase to the current world population. And the larger the compound rate of population growth, the shorter the age on mankind. For example if mankind grows an average three-tenths of one percent yearly, then mankind is less than 9,000 years old.

Yourself: That's a lot less than a million years. What's the explanation for the 990,000 missing years?

Myself: War, famine, and so forth explains some of it, but the two figures are off in power of magnitude: one estimate for mankind's age is 1,000 times larger than the other.

Yourself: So the compound rate for population is all important.

Myself: Exactly. Currently mankind is growing at more than two percent yearly, which means it takes not very long for population to grow. The lowest historical rate I ever heard of was three-tenths of one percent yearly: for that 9 thousand year figure. And a rate below one-tenth of one percent yearly is the mark of a permanently stagnant species, hardly one which would overtake the Earth.

Yourself: But how can they say mankind has been multiplying for a million years or more? There aren't enough people—only five billion of us.

Myself: There's one excuse I can think of, the one you often hear when numbers don't match up.

Yourself: And what's that?

Myself: Rounding error.

Yourself: Rounding?

Myself: Rounding.

Umbertide

So there I stood in Umbertide, which is in Umbria; which is only right, I think.

For a while I rested on the bridge which brings the road in. It jumps a deep canal in its impatience to get there. The ditch is far too big for the trickle of water in it. The stucco backs of a dozen houses are flush with the ditch there, and some of them hang balconies over it to make the most of the air. Below them is one very large poplar growing on a berm, which was glistening in the light the morning I got there. The view was a pastiche of angles and arches, a geometrician's, wonderland. The church called "The Collegial" stood at the end of my view, inviting me into town. A workman chased me out of the church as soon as I entered, with a threat of something about debris falling from the roof where he was working.

Fair enough. At noon it was time to eat, so I hunted the shady little streets among the shops until I found a grocer to give me just what I wanted: a compote of fruits and yogurt, some beans, and a can of sausages, and a chocolate bar. All this I carried down the Romeward way, from which the high hills of Umbria reclined.

The nagging pain had left my one foot. I was almost heartened to find a popping in my other heel instead. So, popping ahead, I made my way through a lowland bent to the Umbrian hills. Mile upon mile I shambled without misadventure (which therefore put me ahead), stopping later to eat my groceries in a roadside glen where I found the porch of a shrine to St. Lucy. From the porch I reclined and admired the regular, the gracious countryside.

Not very far along I came on another shrine, this one to St. Francis. A fence anchored it to its hillside. What caught my eye as I approached was a great cast iron crucifix in the yard like the crucifix found in the Dream of the Rood. It was a modern piece in which the tortured *corpus* had been battered into unity with the cross so that they were indistinguishable one from the other. At first I was annoyed at the artist's liberties with the piece. But there are many ways to praise God and it began to grow on me as I studied it. I think Eric Gill would defend it: the sculptor had looked after Goodness and Truth, and Beauty had looked after herself.

Directly beyond that shrine, a bad thing happened to me. The little Umbrian road which had been nearly mine alone swelled abominably into a four lane highway with trucks and wind and noise. It cut a wide swath down the

middle of the turning valley and avoided every human comfort of villages or shrines. I was mad enough to spit. What's
worse, the road became false; it led me in ways my map
promised it would not. I didn't know where I was. (Distance
I mean, for I knew too well that I was on that freeway.) It
was as though the cartographer had erased a section of my
map and reconnected all the roads and towns differently.

Pining for the villages that I could see against the hills,
and for the conversation that I hadn't enjoyed since the grocer in Umbertide, I pressed along the shoulder of the road.

Sometimes, even with a well-furnished mind, you'll become bored after many long marches and much intellectual
idling. You'll be fresh out of delightful stories, of grave reflections, or hearty songs, or pastoral views to draw, or even
perturbing weather to fight. When you are, you might take to
the last refuge for a weary footman: you might vary the way
you walk.

You'll swing each arm in unison with the leg beneath it
like a stiltwalker so that you torque your spine. Then you'll
make the same movements but with your arms and staff
overhead, like a double metronome, which certainly makes
people stare, and also makes all the blood rush out of your
arms. Then you'll hang your arms and syncopate them at half
the cadence of your legs; but you'll quit this because it's hard
to keep track. Then you'll do the crawl stroke, shooting your
arms before you and behind, and turning your head to
breathe. Then, when the novelty of it all wears off, you'll be
sensible again and walk like a real human being.

Here and there along the road that afternoon were
Italian cypresses, tall and narrow. They're like the Monkey
Trees you used to get by sending in the corn flakes box tops.
You used to get a half-dozen colored crystals in the return
mail. Then you'd put them in water and, right before your
eyes, they grew into narrow colored columns, some of them
green like these cypress trees. Then, when you weren't

looking, your Mom threw them out.

On the other side of the road I read a blue road sign giving the kilometers to Assisi and to Perugia. Of course Assisi was the one which attracted me, and I debated with myself: "Here's the chance which comes too rarely in life, the chance to visit the shrine of a great saint, to step along the streets where he walked. You could go into the town ahead, and ride the bus to Assisi, stay the night there, then return to the march in the morning. Besides, your feet are burning and it would be grand to ride for a while." On the other hand, I thought "my purpose is in Rome and I shouldn't turn from that purpose, whatever the reason, until making the City. A thing nearly done is a thing *not* done." The dilemma plagued my mind for the next five miles.

At the first town within reach I bailed out of that highway. This was Bosco. A bar was conveniently at hand and I took the barman's beer—which was stupid: the wine was cheaper—onto the shaded veranda. Four boys were playing *bocce* in a crude court out front, while two others were throwing a frisbee. I got tickled at their clumsiness with the frisbee. When I finished my beer, I was ready again for the road. But before I left, I showed the boys how to throw their frisbee correctly. "Here, give it a flick with the wrist instead of the elbow. Use your wrist and forget your arm: Like this." It sailed many times farther than before. I was elected. But, being boys, they offered only ice cream so I moved on.

The turn for Assisi led off to the east, that for Perugia drifted west. As I say I'd debated all afternoon: Assisi or not? The moment came. I chose. I stayed on the Romeward way, in keeping with my purpose, but regretted that lane inviting me onto the round hills which hide Assisi from the people of this valley.

Shortly I came off the road and crossed westward into a potato field where the farmer pointed me round by that bridge in the town which vaults the green Tiber there. The

river here is virile and poised, quite unhurried, moving south
in its own good time. More than fifty feet wide, it courts with
some grace the willows which stand near it. Beyond the
bridge, the road eased around through a rising wood which
girdles a hill. On the back side of that hill sat Ponte San Giovanni, the Bridge of St. John.

Ponte San Giovanni

A broad evening light glided down gently onto the
streets as I came up into the town, past its banks and shops. I
found one rugged *pension* up the hill where they gave me
good wine, but wine only. For food I had to hobble back
down the hill by the waning light to a quiet and newer hotel
where I ordered spaghetti, *al dente*, not overcooked.

He told me, did the waiter, that Ponte had once held St.
Francis prisoner as a young man. He also told me that I was
a fool to have bypassed Perugia, the loveliest town
("*bellisima*," with a dip of his hand) in all Umbria. I was, he
said, only 165 kilometers, 100 miles, from Rome. These men
of Ponte lived close enough to the City that they knew casu-

ally of the distance.

Less than a week's walk remained when I rose from my bed in the "Bridge of St. John" to take to the morning again.

I had a problem in my book here: how to describe the country beyond Ponte in an accurate yet interesting way. For though it was Umbria, true enough, it really was not very interesting for the next twenty miles or so: just a lot of wide highway with pottery shops and bars scattered along the road.

And what do you think I did about this problem, Yourself?

Try harder?

Read my horoscope?

Forget it?

Start a chain letter for such descriptions?

Consult the ancients?

See my analyst?

Visit the literately educated?

Consult specialists in prettily describing upper Umbria?

You know very little of such things if you think I did any of these. No. I did what so many wise and thoughtful Americans do when they need authoritative guidance in morals, or in love, or philosophy, or politics, economics, psychology, or—*mirabile dictu*—composition. I wrote to the newspaper.

Dear Delphia,

I never thought I would write to you but I have a problem that I can't discuss with anyone else. I am writing a book about my walk to Rome and I can't think of a pretty way to describe a region which is surprisingly plain and uninteresting for Umbria. There was a gently rolling countryside, and some few villages in it which were unremarkable and had little personality. And all that occupied me was my pushing ahead down the hot two lane roads, and that without interest, for six hours. (Oh, I did pray for a little while in one church I found in a dusty, sun-baked village below the road.)

What should I do? I'm so distraught that I'm working myself into a great trauma.

The Good Egg

Dear Egg,

I'm surprised you haven't thought of the obvious answer. Write an advertisement. This works famously whenever the product to be pushed is difficult. Have a nice day.

Oh, and I wouldn't mention anything about prayer if I were you.

Delphia

But I never wrote that piece after reading this advice. So Yourself must make do with poor this.

About three in the afternoon I ate a roadside meal outside Collazone (very well named for my purpose). It's a little town higher up the hills where my hunger had driven me to look for food and company. Then for more than an hour, I sat in the shade of a chapel near the village and watched two workmen erecting a carnival out of the parts and colors carried on three big trucks. It was ferociously hot and bright, and they worked slowly, unseen by anyone but me. They paced themselves well, as men who are accustomed to heat will do. It was maybe four o'clock before storm clouds came up and I moved on, leaving those men and the two carousels with painted horses now standing on the hillside.

Todi

Cresting a pass back on the highway again, I saw the old city of Todi standing before me, framed by a bridge spanning the road, raised up so very high on its bold hill. Above it moved a roiling black cloud bank. For all the world it looked like that canvas by El Greco, the one called "View of Toledo". In that moment all the earlier insipid hours of that day vanished. I walked ahead into the windy canvas.

The weather was desperate. Lightning shot downward. The wind tore at me, and the rain fell. Directly I made for a steep dirt lane which drove slap up the hill to the town. The pouring water transformed that lane into a mud skid so that walking was harder yet. I needed the whole flats of my feet for better traction on the slippery grade. All that long mile upward I panted and struggled with the incline and the storm. Less a walk than a stair climb, each step took me higher and closer. At five hundred feet up I came through the back gate of the town, between stone pillars glistening in the rain. From here the road was asphalt, but just as steep. Beyond those gates the road bore the name of the Street of the Pewter Tears of El Greco (*Strada del Lagrime Peltro de El Greco*, the sign said). Upwards I came in my poncho, digging with my staff, past the houses clinging to that fierce high hill, and along the upended streets of old Todi. The slippery footing stopped me several times, nearly tipping me over as it twisted its way upwards between houses darkened by the rain. Some few people there watched me haul my carcass higher; a few nodded, but none helped. Still I outlasted the hilly pavement and at last entered that ancient cobblestone plaza where those two palaces sit before the town's cathedral.

They have a bishop in Todi, but they have no water pressure. Still in the scheme of things necessary for happiness, that puts them in good shape. Around the corner from the plaza I found a hotel room at a high price, a pretty case of market segmentation by hoteliers if you ask me.

The owner's wife presiding at her desk was passing time with a younger woman, slender and dark and somewhat pleasing in manner, who had arrived from the island of Sardinia. It took very little coaxing to get the story of my pilgrimage once I'd stopped breathing hard. To their questions I gave answers of some honesty, but there was embellishment as well. We three sat in the front room which served as our parlor, trading stories of our travels around Europe, the business of the hotel now forgotten for a time.

Somewhere in the conversation the younger woman made an invitation: "When you get to Rome, maybe you would like to visit Sardinia. A boat is available from Ostia Lido, just outside Rome on the coast. It takes just three hours for the boat to reach the island, and Olbia my town.

Sardinia is very pretty in May now. Perhaps you could come."

That was charming of her to invite me to her island. But my business after all was in Rome. "Perhaps," I said, "if I have money and time when I've reached the City. Perhaps. Thank you!" She wrote her name and address and gave it to me.

After the rain stopped I went outside to see the town. On the square, under the arcade of one of the palaces, I found a small crowd beside several tables full of pamphlets. Activists in the Radical party were gathered there.

Yourself: Off the pigs! Up the Revolution! Peace now! Power to the people!

Myself: What was all that?

Yourself: I'm the People: the Chorus. I'm just getting into the mood. Please go on.

Myself: Their speaker was a soft-spoken, bespectacled, honest-looking bourgeois woman, like Simone Weil in her photographs, a woman seemingly thoughtful and thus all the more persuasive. She answered my questions with no emotion at first. But I baited her and pretty soon we were arguing about her condemnation of hunting and her praise of abortion. She refused to admit the idiocy of her notions. Parrying with her a little in English I found it with her as with other Aliens who hate life: I was dealing not with an intellect in honest defense of truth, but with a belly, a cluster of wants, and a willful rejection of known truth: an Albigensian. Her wrong-headedness was all too common. She was one of those who rail against water damage at the Chicago Fire. It helps them think well of themselves.

I declared that I was her enemy—which only made her shrug—and crossed the square, to a dogleg alley which looked like one of Piranesi's prison scenes. I descended there to a weathered house near the bottom reach of the town, a house in the Etruscan bones of Todi. Inside I got hot spaghetti by the bowl and red wine and a quiet hour in which to think. There was a fine fire burning in a grate which warmed me and kept at bay the dark chills stalking outside.

Todi

The more I thought about her the more the woman outside vexed me. She should have been ashamed of herself: peddling bourgeois rot and death instead of counseling wisdom and hope, and mercy. Shame on her and on all Aliens like her. Shame on her.

Maybe the fire was of hickory wood, if there are hickory trees in Italy. It popped a lot. But then if it had been hickory, there would have been barbecue at hand. And there was no barbecue. Anyway. The deeper I looked into the fire and the more I pieced on that spaghetti, the more I valued an observation by Edith Stein: that modern Europeans live as lapsed Catholics with bad consciences.

I remembered too that Todi resembled Toledo, which reminded me of the marvelous poet Roy Campbell in Toledo

during the Spanish Civil War. The Nationalists (whom the
Alien woman in the square above would certainly applaud)
had been elected and had begun a rampage of the countryside, murdering priests and nuns, sacking convents and
monasteries and burning churches. Owning a missal was
good for a death sentence. A community of Carmelites near
the Campbells' home had several times used the house to
hide monks from slaughter by the Reds. (For this, Campbell
was confirmed secretly by the very Primate of Spain.) On
one occasion the monks brought to the Campbells the
papers of St. John of the Cross in a trunk for safekeeping.
Just days later, this same community of Carmelites,
seventeen of them, were slaughtered in the church yard by
the Nationalist Reds, covered with a tarpaulin, and left there
while their library was put to the torch. It burned for several
days. Every morning the Campbells would look from their
house toward that library to see if the cross atop it ever fell.
It never did. The martyrdom of the Carmelites by the
Popular Front inspired Roy Campbell and Mary until the
end of their lives, they said. After that, he became an even
more confirmed Catholic, an advocate of Franco; he was
unwilling to tolerate the received judgments of the
bourgeoisie concerning the Spanish Civil War.

Such things I considered sadly until the house closed
and I was put out into a soft, European rain to climb the
night street to the square, then across it in front of the
cathedral to my room.

Not many hours later, in a foggy morning glimmer I re-
crossed the empty square to the cathedral to get Mass. I
even beat the sexton to church. He found me trying the great
front doors and led me around by the side entrance. With
the few minutes I had, I prowled the nave until Mass, which
a dozen of us heard. And then I was off through Todi for the
city gate below.

On the other side of town, not far from the square, I

found the city's second church, whose facade is unfinished these past several centuries. The signs inside the church directed me to an underground crypt and the brown sarcophagus which sits behind an iron grill. An old woman was washing the crypt floor. Beside her was the tomb of Jacopone da Todi.

Franciscan Cross in Todi

Jacopone was born in 1230, four years after the death of St. Francis. He died in 1306, in Collazzone, where I ate that lunch while the carnival was being erected, preceding

Dante in this by some 15 years. Until the age of 38 he was an accomplished lawyer and a happy husband. In that year sudden disaster struck. His young wife, Vanna, fell from a balcony at a public festival and was mortally injured. When Jacopone ran to unlace her to find her injuries, he discovered for the first time that she wore haircloth next to her skin. She died; he became foolish. Wealthy, he became poor. Being learned, he became ignorant. Formerly worldly, carnal, and avaricious, he became a poet of poverty, a Franciscan tertiary, and a *beato*. He wrote his *Canzoniere* in the Umbrian dialect, poems whose greatness Frederick Ozanam first discovered, outside Italy, and twenty-five generations have ratified. Papini named Jacopone "the greatest religious poet of the Italian Middle Ages, one of the greatest poets in the world." Because of this same poetry, Papini wrote that "nothing greater has ever been known in this world, among human works, then Sanctity expressed in Beauty." It was this *beato*, poet of sanctity, who lay in that sarcophagus in Todi.

The road dropped out of old Todi like a wounded gray dove, shot at morning and falling through the bright haze. It flapped downward, bringing me with it until I was away from the beaming town above. Below, I had to choose my way to Rome, which now lay but three days off. On my map, a scribble of road wended mostly south for Rome, but it lay across ample hills with a promise of serious struggle in them. Another line veered southeast around these hills, a gentleman's cruise to Rome. The former promised to be the last hill mass of all my long marches to Rome, so onto the twisted hill road I came.

It was a kick in the head, that road, mounting hill upon greater hill. Spreads of fir woods and broadleaf were gathered beside an apron of vineyards or fields upon the lap of Umbria. Elsewhere there were things more familiar to me: alfalfa, and fields of sunflowers, which give an oil for cooking. A fine bright sun left me panting and hot, but happy to be exerting myself. Upward I climbed, toward the sun for a good couple of hours. What few cars there were had to strain too hard at the road themselves to bother with harassing me.

Pesciano

Two tiny, shining clutches of houses were strung onto that road like solitary pearls. In the second of these, I called between pants to an old woman working behind the fence of her home.

"How far is Sismano?" I asked. All the early signs had been of Sismano, but they'd vanished the past few miles.

"*Parite. Sismano parite,*" she declared, brushing at me with the back of her hand, returning to her gardening.

I thanked her with a nod so that she'd think me self-assured, but once I was out of sight I stopped and fished out my dictionary. I rubbed my head. I didn't understand what she'd told me.

There were two possible spellings of the word she'd

given. The one, *parita*, I construed to mean "the same distance as you've come.". But from where: Todi? Bolzano? Schesslitz? I was puzzled. I looked at the other spelling, *parete*. This one alarmed me: it meant "wall", as in "take it to the wall".

I wondered and walked upward past the silver leafs of the olive groves. As if on cue, the asphalt dropped sharply twice and I veered east around a hillside of pines before it climbed up steeply in the midday heat and brought me sweating and squinting in front of the hamlet Sismano upon its hill. I found it sitting there like a grand, pale nautilus curled upward along one stone street and hemmed in by a skirt of rock.

Sismano

Sismano is a jewel. If its people were of a mind, they might become the littlest state, perhaps a principality, smaller even than San Marino or the Vatican. Sismano has nearly everything a republic or statelet might need: boundaries, a tavern, a grocer, a wood wright, families, a church, children, and even gentry. I wonder what stops them from declaring their independence.

I admired it from the road and as I came through its one gate, shadowed by two little boys. Above me, near the gate, a dark haired woman leaning out of her window smiled and assured me there was a bar. One of the little boys showed me the cellar which housed the bar, but it was closed. A workman in another cellar who saw us quit his lathe and all that sawdust, and sent the boy for the barman.

Presently he arrived, a tall distinguished old gentleman who smiled courteously and showed me into his cellar where it was so cool. He let in some light by the open door, shooed away the little boy, and unfastened a window shutter across the room. The old gentleman took his place behind a counter and asked me my pleasure.

"Wine," I said.

"There is no wine just now," he apologized.

"Then I'll have beer, please."

He opened a bottle and poured it for me.

"Seltzer too? in the beer?" he asked.

It was good. We began talking of the weather, he and I, because we were both civilized. Neither of us sat at one of the half dozen tables, but rather we stood at the counter. I knew he'd only opened the bar to accommodate me. So though I drank slowly and savoured both of those beers, I tried not to tarry or impose upon his time. We talked briefly of his relatives in Pennsylvania, but he couldn't remember the name of their town. Then, my beers finished, I took my leave of him, each of us having done the other good. That's how it should be in this world: doing one another good.

He came out with me and locked the cellar door, leaving me with a *"bon diurno"* to stand in the one shining street of Sismano. Making my way around and up by the street I came upon two delights. Two of them. There are marvels in even the slightest parts of God's world. At the top of the

street I found first a church, and then a palace. I was confronted at the side door of the church by a surly carpenter
who was suspicious of me. He told me to go away and closed
the door in my face. So I walked around the front of the
church and up to the terrace of the palace which is next
door.

The rich we have ever with us. There were as many
rooms in that palace, I think, as in all the rest of Sismano: it
was four stories tall. The windows rose upon three sides of a
courtyard. A white Alfa Romeo sat to one side of the terrace, the side which presented a belvedere to the same Umbrian hills through which I'd marched earlier that day. To the
opposite side of the terrace stood grillwork and a gate, and
beyond the gate was a tiled courtyard, ill kept. There were
plants here and there which had gone to seed. A staircase
led up to the entrance on the second floor whereby the rich
people who live there come and go, but not until after a
climb nor before a drop (which is justice, I think). The palace
was wearing tolerably, like old money does, but it was not in
the best of repair. Smart money says the little church will be
there when the family of the palace has become a memory.

A lush pine tree grew outside by the gate of the town.
Beneath it I sat down to draw and to eat in the shade, to
watch first one lone woman and then two more walk by me
at a distance to size me up. A pigeon cooed faintly somewhere; cicadas sawed away in the hot, dry, afternoon grass.
The air drifted this way and that, without purpose. By and
by, as I was finishing my lunch, two white oxen passed on the
road, dragging a wooden cart loaded with old hay, for the
new hay in the fields wasn't yet ready for cutting. A dark
man about my own age, in shirt sleeves and a cap, slumped in
the seat, riding toward Avigliano. I followed him away
through the sunlight.

The day was a pretty good one for walking though less
good for climbing. Clouds tempered the strong sun on and

off. The sky was very bold wherever it was blue. The hills were behind me for now. Walking in the sunlight was sweat-bringingly hot; walking in the shade was cool. The grasses and the trees waved companionably, each celebrating its place on the face of Umbria.

Umbria is a poem. Everything in Umbria is placed. Nowhere do you find jumbles of color nor of emotion. Nothing there is random. Rather each field, each tree or house, each hedge or road is placed where it belongs, in ensemble. So too the sky. And each is distinct. The whole effect is that of a poem, crafted first and then colored, and placed where it might be recited by man.

I came along easily from Sismano to where I could see Avigliano town a mile or so ahead, gathered around its Florentine church tower. I mean a mile or so by line of sight, because the road took an outlandish dogleg out of all proportion through a cemetery before it turned for the town.

Sometimes I'm very clever. Sometimes not. This day I was not.

The little valley between me and Avigliano looked easy, so I left the road. I slipped down a slope of loose, weedy slag which rolled downhill before me. Below this, what had looked to be a tree line beside a stream proved to be a thorn and bramble barricade astride a miserable little runnel choked with vines. Though it was only twenty yards wide, I was ten minutes hacking and cursing and splashing and bleeding my way through it. My pack nearly didn't make it through there with me: it came unhooked at the belt and hung only upon one sore elbow as I emerged. In using my staff to clear thorns, I gashed my hand. From there it was a slippery ascent across two muddy fields of young oats, as farm dogs barked at me from a hill to the west; then an instantaneous pratfall into a hole as deep as my staff; next a cursed slog through more mud higher up. I was ready for that sweet red wine which they keep in Avigliano, wine like sherry almost, I don't know where from. I should have guessed that the folks in Sismano would have marked the easiest route there.

Pond Before Amelia

Beyond Avigliano the road dropped down all over again and then pitched left in front of that high hill on which sits, like a vulture, the old town that sits there. Before me lay the floor of a charming and orderly valley, absolutely flat, absolutely, and filled with its fair grasses and pastures and a number of good vines. And all along it to the high west and front were tall, regular Umbrian hills dressed in pine woods, with lesser hills facing them to the east. Mirroring these hills in the east were low olive groves with their silvery leaves stilled in the air. A young man leading two white ewes on a chain passed me where I stood: I looking into the valley and knowing that I must deal with the great hills at the valley's end. I paced behind him at a respectful distance and then quickened my walk slightly when he led the ewes from the road onto a berm to graze.

The whole of that herdsman's valley was at rest, overarched by a placid sky so far away that it had lost every color.

An influence of serenity, an air or a suggestion of that repose which is like the beatitudes lingered in the grass below those hushed old hills, those constant hills, catching the whole of that day in the embrace which we may imagine of innocence. The pastoral charm of the valley and of that league where I passed southward were the more vivid for having been unannounced. Men have done good and human things in that valley since before the days which any among us remembers. And the effect has remained. Lovely little hidden valley of Umbria. Charming little Avenue of the Embrace of All Innocence. *Via del Abbraccio de Innocenza Intera*. And so it is.

But at the end of that valley the rising and the winding began again. I had no warning of a village on the hillside until I rounded a curve and found it there among the trees. From there it was a sharp rise, and a push, onto the breast of those deep western woods I'd seen from the valley. After a tough hike of seven miles, the road threaded through the timbers and then dropped down again into a second valley and the pestilence of traffic leading to Amelia.

At the first house where I stopped, the woman sent me packing: something about the sweat or the grime, the smell or maybe the stubble or the staff put her off. At the second house I was accepted, and good luck it was: the grandmother who owned it was renowned locally for her cooking. She had newspaper articles on the wall from as far away as Baltimore to prove it. The wine was good as were the bread and bean soup. But I was disappointed by the roast chicken. It was tough and dry and quite small. Upon such fragile evidence rests the fame of others. An older couple at a nearby table who were French thought it looked very good, and volunteered approving nods or hums while I ate. But then they also thought it was pigeon. They were French.

Sleep in that house was fine once it came. But before I slept I paused to compose myself. I was now two days from the City, two days' walk from discharging my pilgrimage. The effort and prayers of so many days afoot, the perseverance through so many seasons had brought me very close. God willing, the night after next I would sleep in the City. God willing.

Amelia

A beaming chill stiffened the morning of my leave-taking from Amelia. The high sunlight caromed off the ancient limestone of Amelia, its walls begun in the 6th Century before Christ. Some of this cold light shattered and imbedded itself in the rock as shards so that the street was glare-bright on the side nearest the walls. Across from the gates, on the southern side, was a tree-shadowed row of shops where I changed the last of my money and bought my provisions for the days: rolls, some sausages, cheese, an apple, some pear juice.

Pretty green meadows lay upon the hills I passed, and also lines of maples along their borders. Throughout the first of these meadows my road travelled downward a little, on a twisting way, then onto the backs of lesser hills. I was on the descent to Rome now. I could feel it in the road.

There weren't any true villages along the way that morning. None. There were just rumpled hay fields and farmyards and dense ranks of elms or maples. One farmyard on my right held a herd of thirty or more beef cattle, a breed of shorthorn it seemed, the first herd of any size I'd seen in days. Falling more than rising, the road brought me downwards. Two workmen were laboring in the heat to mow the roadside grass with a two-wheeled cutter. The smaller of the two, bare chested, wrestled the snarling mower this way and that while the bigger fellow (the chief) went ahead to kick away debris. All the while the road dropped or twisted, like a huge gray bull at the end of a rodeo ride. It led me past lush corn fields, and then collapsed, after a morning grown quite hot, onto the grasses beneath Orte.

Orte itself clung to its crag beside the road, the better to stare into Latium which began beyond. The town was off my path and a good thing too: it's packed onto a high stone hill with its homes crowded right up to the edge of the drop. The road onto that rock looked to be pure trouble. Here and there church towers stood above the massed roofs. Some of the smaller buildings seemed to have been pushed off the hilltop by their larger cousins. They lay scattered about the green apron of the rock. In one of these lower places, a grocer's, I bought some more rolls and some pressed pork to eat later. The things I'd bought in Amelia were gone already. But there were other hungers in me which couldn't be satisfied by meat and drink.

Somewhere near Orte I rejoined the Tiber, finding it on my eastern side. There we two left Umbria and passed into Latium. The province of the city now passed beneath my feet. I began to swagger, to carry myself with pride and ease deeper into the now level province until I made Orte Scalo, which is a lesser place, hardly a village in the true sense.

There was a striped (or "hooped," for the pedant) Romanesque church in the town with a brilliant entablature of mosaics. It's like Orvieto's yet far less grand. But then most entablatures are less grand than Orvieto's. The picture is of Our Lord with His arms opened to us. The crisp blues and golds, the clean greens and mauve present Christ Pantocrator. Those hooped walls, with their alternate courses of rose and gray stone, gave the whole church a leap out at one.

At the very edge of town, just beyond the church, a bald, stocky man passed me on a motorbike, dismounted, and hailed me from a gate beside the road.

"You must be weary. It's hot on this road. That sun is very bad. I have some wine you would like. I know you would. Come and sit down over there and I'll bring it." It was the gate of his own house. He was courteous to me and I was curious.

Now perseverance is a good thing; but it isn't *every* good thing. I left the road. He sat me down on a bench near a brick shed where we could watch the road. Through the shed door when he went in, I saw a dark cellar absolutely choked with wine bottles. There were great four-hand jugs in wicker baskets, small ten-noggin bottles, and one huge tun which he claimed held two hundred litres of wine. And all of it bold and strong. He had upwards of two hundred gallons in there.

Yourself: Now, there's your red wine, and your white and (as the waitress said) your pink. Which had you?

Myself: The red. The same as he.

Yourself: A very good choice.

Myself: We sat with our wine and he told me of his life as a young soldier: fighting the Russians in the snow at first, then fighting alongside the Allies. He'd been astonished at how well the American and British troops had travelled. He and the other Italians had struggled along with whatever had been at hand. Perhaps that's why he couldn't understand my walking to Rome.

"Why don't you just buy a ticket on the train or the bus?" he asked disgustedly with great waves of the arms. "You have money don't you? Don't go through all this nonsense of walking. You could be in Rome in an hour." I answered noncommittally and worked on that wine with no name.

He thought I was unbalanced. I knew that the meaning of my pilgrimage escaped him, because he scolded me for not riding. Well I didn't need that and so I left him there, his red wine reduced by one day's ration.

The Tiber rolled along beyond a strip of meadow where I walked. In the middle of the afternoon, thunderheads gathered without notice and whipped up a sudden downpour. It forced me from the road for an hour. Then it all ended and let me hurry behind it along the steaming pavement, pining for Rome, anxious to see her face. She now lay less than fifty miles away.

Via Flaminia

At the crossing of a tiny stream I found a graven block of granite beneath one ancient elm. Up shot my heart! Upon that block were carved two words. *"VIA FLAMINIA."* It was the Roman road! Rome herself had built the way from here, in the age of Hannibal. She was no mere rumor now. She was mistress of this district: she'd set this ancient road herself. The pavement was modern but the cut for the road was ancient. How many pilgrims for how many centuries have found the Flaminian Way and worn it in their hurry? How many more in the centuries to come will happen upon this marker. It was good to touch that stone.

The Flaminian Way sprang like the young child Hope onto the upland and then rambled with me for miles, full of ease and a great confidence.

Up there I found an inn beside the road. I entered to celebrate and to prepare myself to appear in the presence of the City.

She, *inamorata*, was now but one day's march away. With one last manly effort I could bring myself to Her. I could redeem my pledge.

I slept very little that last of all those many nights. And I rose early that final morning, tired but very eager to be off. When I stepped out of doors I found a horrendous downpour which destroyed the early light so that, though it was past seven of a June morning, it looked to be four A.M. in March. Nothing is more irksome to any man afoot than rain. But I would not wait. I made a prayer on the porch of the inn while I shouldered my pack and arranged my poncho against the water. I asked for one more day's protection and strength. I pulled the hood over my head, and I took the road this last time as a pilgrim for Rome.

There was no dawn, behind that ferocious rain. Above the land there was only a cowering, timid glow. It was a march through outlands of grief and desolation.

Would you think that in such a storm you were to be able to see? You would not see, except the lightning and the few cars hurtling headlights at you with disregard. Would you think you were to hear? No, there would be nothing reaching your ears but the roar of the water or the thunder. And what of your body? Would you hope for warmth or ease in such a downpour? You could not hope, for the cold and the blowing water were everywhere, especially in your boots. Your poncho was nearly useless, and this for pitiless mile after mile. The road itself would buck and dive, and climb, and channel rainwater, but you would pound onward. Only determination and quarrels with Heaven would bring you into Rignano after three dark hours in that debilitating rain.

At my first opportunity I took shelter in a pretentious bar restaurant where the keeper first frowned and then ignored me. I admit I wasn't much to see. I sat there at a table just inside the dining room changing my socks. He sent one surly young woman to bring me bad white wine at a dear price. I drank his wretched wine and left him to it after voicing my complaint. Since I was on the last day of my pilgrimage I trust my displeasure had special effect. No other house in all of Rignano would serve me. Two of them turned me out into the storm, telling me they weren't open yet. Blast them! I set my face south against the rain and hammered on into drowning, writhing Latium.

Briefly, say for no more than twenty minutes, the rain stopped somewhere beyond the town and the sky brightened as though there were sunshine somewhere. Just then, at hand I saw a span of flat stones in the earth which I understood at once. Beside the asphalt, under a line of firs, were the broad and fitted stones of the *Via*, laid by the Romans twenty-two centuries ago. Onto those wetted stones I walked. I felt the purchase in my legs of those ancient marching legions which once passed beneath the pines and made so much of what became Europe, and of those thousands who came to hear Peter and Paul and then carried home the Truth.

Via Flaminia

Then it began again. It was hard rain that fell on me. Hard and loud. The lightning flashed fiercely on all sides. Water fell and water ran. Water covered the ground. It shut out the sky. Wind-driven water; abusive water; brutal water, cold, rushing, soaking water. Rain and yet more rain. Rain like Noah knew. Rain primeval. Not a shower, but rain pure and bold. Rain to wound a man. Hitting, hurting, beating, flashing rain. Bullying rain. Punishing rain. Painful rain. Rain for drowning the blaze in a man's heart. Lord, will there ever again be such a rain?

I was forced from the road again, weakened, into a bar where I could eat under shelter. The power was off in there. I stood dripping in the dark beside two other men and cursed the water which had plagued me now for five hours. All that the others would say was that a man was a fool to be out walking in it. Unashamed, I crossed myself there by the doorway and prayed for a stop to the rain. Not two minutes later the storm ended. I was off, with a snap of my fingers at the clouds. It was a good example for the others to follow.

You can't hesitate to use your authority, if necessary, when you're a pilgrim to Rome. Nor should you be surprised when it works.

I was still peevish because a cold breeze was working its way into my clothing. An Enemy had made this last day of my journey a trial. What's more, the weaving road underfoot reeled from hillock to soggy hillock, troubling both itself and me to look into all the little corners of Latium as though Rome were the farthest thing from its asphalt mind. I'd thought the *Via Flaminia* this near to Rome would be direct and exact. My heart was set on the house of the Fisherman, and home.

The sun struggled with the dark vapors overhead. I took sides and cheered the sun on, but hedged my bet all the same by squishing ahead. Sunlight ebbed or flowed, and the outcome was often in doubt. But with one bold, deft blaze the good sun scorched a clean breach in the clouds, just above where I thought Rome to lie. The sky shattered into pieces, and all that blue light which lays beyond this poor world came pouring through.

At this the day was won. The vapors fell away from the

fiery star and there was the day all about me. Sunshine lay upon a glistening earth. My way, the Flaminian Way, was straight now and descending, with stout trees to either side, though the land was falling away to southward and to west.

At first I doubted. I thought it an image. I thought myself still too far off to catch sight of her. But I strained nonetheless and stood on my toes. I peeked between the tops of the trees below me. And then I knew.

There, from the *Via Flaminia*, I saw St. Peter's, standing in light some miles off and below me. And all around Her, attending Her as is Her due, I saw the City.

I had won!

My heart convulsed in a burst of laughter. The Devil's back snapped with a mighty crack. She who had denied me so very long had, in Her own time, yielded at last. Trembling and laughing, and crying only a little, I looked down upon the loveliness of Rome. In no way can I gather for you onto this page the names of all the joys, mortal and spiritual, which crowded my heart when I saw Her.

It's hard for us that our loves be tested, but it's good that they endure. We who make our way in the company of the Faith yield to so many things which serve to turn us from our purpose. Our devotion grows lax, and our consciences cloud from the assault of our sins, and we fashion of our lives such things as we had not wished. She alone in all our hard passage remains shining and true. She alone is faithful. She alone is who She was when She first came to us from His hand. She alone does not betray us, nor abandon us in the dark ways. She burns the lamp for us by evening and spreads the feast upon Her altars.

I had done badly what I had so wanted to do well. I had gotten many things wrong and the right things only by parts. And I had mistaken courtesy for affection. But I had carried myself and my burden across Europe to the porch of that house where we the living have our Home.

By 9:30 I came to the city walls, just a mile from the Basilica. Strangely, the need to help find a woman traveler lodgings for the night led me away from the walls, to a hotel on the far side of the Tiber, and then to a grassy lawn where I slept my last sleep, but this one in Rome.

Piazza del Popolo

It was Saturday and it was the finest morning I yet saw come into the world. I strode proudly down the last of the Flaminian Way and through the brick walls of Rome by the Piazza del Popolo, where sit those twin churches to either side. I followed off by a street which led past the *Ara Pacis*, for which I did not stop, and then onto a bridge to my right which crossed the Tiber for the last time. Beyond the *Castel Santangelo* I came onto the *Via Conciliazione*, the Street of Conciliation. It was crowded with my brother and sister pilgrims, their buses and their taxis. Above the crowds I saw the face of the Basilica before me. Grinning, I thrust that worn old staff skyward and praised God! *Exsultet*!

I straightened my back and carried solemnly toward Her, eyes fixed on Her. My mind was numb, but my soul was ablaze as I entered that marvel of a plaza. Once again I raised my staff overhead to Her, grasping it at either end, saluting the Mother of Men.

Regretting my execrable sins with all of my heart, I stepped forward under the portico, and to my right toward the Holy Door. Gently I placed a kiss upon it, then turned, and walked inside.

The many peoples of the earth were represented there in St. Peter's. There were Germans, Frenchmen, and Englishmen, some Brazilians, plenty of Italians, Poles (and these were all crying), Africans, Japanese, Indian nuns wearing the habit of Mother Teresa, Arabs, and at least one American. And the Pope himself—that magnificent Pole—celebrated Mass for us in martyr's red.

St. Peter's

Now we're to part, Yourself. We've served one another well, though you haven't always kept up your end of the conversation. And when the dogs were loosed at us I had reason to doubt you. But we both have prevailed.

If my patience with you were less than it has been, I might more than once have given you the slip and let you find your own way to Rome. But then were your devotion less than mine, you wouldn't have come with me, and I would have been alone, a terrible thing to suffer.

So I'll say goodnight to you here in St. Peter's and leave you to your own in Rome. I ask you to remember me. For I think we will meet one another again, if not soon then surely at the Judgment.

And perhaps it will not be so very long until that hour of our reunion. For they tell me that this pretty world is ending. That's what they say: this pretty, pretty world is ending.

Yourself: Are we there yet?